BOOKS BY THE SAME AUTHOR

Landings (2009)
Field Notes (Volume One) (2012)*
Moor Glisk (2012)
Limnology (2012)
Nimrod is lost in Orion and
Osyris in the Doggestarre (2014)
Memorious Earth (2015)*
Beyond the Fell Wall (2015)
The Pale Ladder (Selected Poems
& Texts 2009–2014) (2016)
Towards a Frontier (2017)
The Look Away (2018)
Dark Hollow Dark (2019)
LASTGLACIALMAXIMUM (2020)
And Then Gone (2020)

* with Autumn Richardson

A FLINT INCENTIVE

RICHARD SKELTON

SELECTED POEMS & TEXTS

(2015–20)

XYLEM BOOKS 2020

XY01 The Look Away (2018)

XY02 Field Notes (Volume One) (2018)

XY03 Heart of Winter (2018)

XY04 The Pale Ladder (2018)

XY05 Memorious Earth (2018)

XY06 Landings (2019)

XY07 Living In The World As If It Were Home (2019)

XY08 Moosewood Sandhills (2019)

XY09 An Almost-Gone Radiance (2020)

XY10 And Then Gone (2020)

XY11 A Flint Incentive (2020)

XY12 Limnology (2020)

Richard Skelton, *A Flint Incentive*, Selected Poems & Texts, 2015–2020

1:1

ISBN: 978-1-9163935-2-3

Xylem Books is an imprint of Corbel Stone Press

FROM *Ferae Naturae* (2015)

The Not-Fire (2015)

The Medicine Earth (2015)

FROM *Beyond the Fell Wall* (2015)

The Men Have Gone (2015)

FROM *The Cult Revived* (2015–20)

End Matter

for Autumn

FERAE NATURAE

EXCERPTS | 2015

INTRODUCTION

The manuscripts presented in these *Findings* were brought to the attention of the Notional Research Group for Cultural Artefacts by artist Richard Skelton, who discovered them among the Collingwood Archive at Abbot Hall Art Gallery, Kendal. According to Skelton, the manuscripts were found within an envelope from Faber & Gwyer Ltd, date-stamped 7.15pm, May 21st, 1926. The envelope also contained a 'Memorandum of Agreement' between Faber & Gwyer Ltd and W.G. Collingwood, stamped with the same date, for the publication of his book entitled *Northumbrian Crosses of the Pre-Norman Age*.

The manuscripts comprise two signatures (hereafter identified as UXDI-1 and UXDI-2) removed from the *Transactions of the Cumberland and Westmorland Antiquarian and Archaeological Society*, Volume XV, 1898 (a publication which Collingwood himself edited between 1901 and 1925). UXDI-1 comprises ten pages, four of which are text (numbered 163 to 166) and three plates (numbered II to IV), the reverse of which contain writing in black ink. Pages 163 and 164 also contain a small amount of marginalia. UXDI-2 comprises four unnumbered pages, two of which are plates (IX and X), one 'to face p. 268' and the other 'to face p. 269'. One of the plates contains writing in black ink. The other three are unadorned.

In total there are eleven titled (underlined) and two untitled texts. They have been reproduced here as faithfully as possible, with italics substituted for the underlined text. (Square brackets denote words where the original handwriting is unclear.) The subject of the manuscripts themselves is the historic persecution of animal life in old Cumberland and Westmorland, set against a series of mythological, folkloric and historical vignettes depicting animal veneration from pre-Roman times until the late Middle-Ages. We have since undertaken an examination of the Collingwood Archive at Abbot Hall, and can find no reference to the manuscripts themselves, nor can we find any indication that Collingwood himself enquired into such a theme. His own attitude to animal persecution can perhaps be summed up in an excerpt from his *Lake District History* in which he discusses the 'pretty sport' of fox-hunting. Whilst we have therefore been unable to establish the provenance and authenticity of the manuscripts themselves, we can at least say that they are not the product of Collingwood's hand.

In conjunction with the publication of these *Findings*, a temporary 'Museum of Feræ Naturæ' was housed at Abbot Hall in 2015, exhibiting the manuscripts themselves along with a series of artefact assemblages selected by Richard Skelton, in collaboration with the NRGCA, which explore the idea of 'the double-life of banal objects', as referenced in manuscript UXDI-I.

As the phrase 'double life' suggests, the aim in re-presenting these objects was not to deny their ostensible purpose, but to hint at other ways in which they could be viewed and used.

The reference to plague and famine cults of the late Middle-Ages in UXDI-1 therefore created a context for these artefacts to be percieved as discrete ritual objects: everyday items improvised into temporary religious assemblages. A plumb-bob became the face of a hare; a wool-comb, the horns of a bull-deity; a pair of wool-shears became the ears of a wolf-fox, and another, intersecting it, became its open jaws.

These artefacts were sourced from the collection of the Museum of Lakeland Life and Industry, and the collection of Kendal Museum. We would like to extend particular thanks to Nick Rogers and James Arnold from Lakeland Arts, for their open-minded co-operation in producing this exhibition and accompanying publication. We would also like to thank Carol Davies from Kendal Museum, and Rhys Trimble for his assistance in translating the Welsh words within the manuscripts.

Palimpsest: Commenta Bernensia.
Made of the calf. Oak gall on flayed skin.
Words cluster around a network of veins.
cf. Lucherno: fox-boy, Copper Prince.
Dreams of the threefold death.
Hanged, throat cut, plunged in water.
Teutates appeased. Esus appeased. Taranis appeased.
Dwells in the ground face down.
Vulpes on his neck. Skin on skin.
'Llwynog fyddi'n tywyswr i'r ddaear dan ddaear.'

[UXDI-I]

[**COMMENTA BERNENSIA**] A gloss on a 10th century Bern manuscript that expands upon descriptions of druidic rituals in Lucan's epic poem *Pharsalia*. [**LUCFERNO**] cf. *luφerno-, 'fox' (Proto-Celtic). [**COPPER**] Some elements of this 'ritual death' accord with that of Lindow Man, discovered in Cheshire, England, in 1984. Lindow Man, a so-called bog body, was found to have been the subject of *overkill*, and to have elevated levels of copper on his skin. [**THREEFOLD DEATH**] Killed in three different ways, with possible symbolic overtones. John Rhys, in his *Lectures on the Origin and Growth of Religion as illustrated by Celtic Heathendom* (1892), commented on the trifold nature of the Celtic deity Cernunnos, who is sometimes depicted with three faces or heads: 'the Autun figure [a representation of Cernunnos] combined all his most salient attributes, the horns, the three faces, the cross-legged posture, the torque round his neck, and another resting on his lap and separating two ram-headed serpents.' (p. 94). [**TEUTATES / ESUS / TARANIS**] It is possible to view the subjects of overkill as offerings to three different gods. According to the *Commenta Bernensia*, dedications to Teutates were drowned, those to Esus were hanged and those to Taranis were burned. [**VULPES**] *Vulpes vulpes*, the common fox. Lindow Man was found naked except for a fox-fur arm covering. [**LLWYNOG FYDDI'N ... DDAEAR**] We have been unable to trace the provenance of this line written in the Welsh language, which translates as: 'Fox be my guide to the earth beneath earth'. It is perhaps worth noting that, in the late Iron Age, the inhabitants of what is now Cumbria would have spoken an ancient antecedent of the Welsh language. The animal as psychopomp is not without precedent in mythology.

Apotropaism: cf. still life of the dismembered head.
Pins and piss in bottles. The horseshoe as a charm
more powerful than the cross.
St. Dunstan shepherd thy flock.
Sent feebly to bring the [errant] into the [fold].
Full soon Nyke's silent wonder broke.
The endurance of iron. Still seen above doors
and mantles where the rood has long
                                        since rotted.
An analogue—a vestige—of the horns of
                                        Cernunnos.

[UXDI-I]

[APOTROPAISM] Averting evil or bad luck through the use of ritual, often involving charmed objects. [STILL LIFE] A possible reference to the significance of the head within pre-Christian Celtic culture. [PINS AND ... BOTTLES] Most likely a reference to the witch bottle, an apotropaic device thought to afford protection from witchcraft. Such objects were often hidden within walls to protect a dwelling. [ST. DUNSTAN] The fable of 'St. Dunstan and the Devil' can be seen as an attempt to assimilate superstitious beliefs surrounding the horseshoe into Christian orthodoxy. [FULL SOON ... BROKE] Excerpt: *The Horse-Shoe, the True Legend of St. Dunstan and the Devil,* Edward G. Flight (1871), p. 36. [CERNUNNOS] The first direct reference to this Celtic horned god, whom John Rhys discussed at length in *Lectures on the Origin and Growth of Religion as illustrated by Celtic Heathendom* (1892).

A Necklace for St. Bega: Beghoc.
Maiden of the moor, beached on our coast
and made here her retreat. The hidden path:
her armilla found in the collar of a lowly beast,
freed from chains, worn about her virgin neck,
jewelled with nails.
'Hir swire is whiter thann the swann.'
Meat she did not take, but fasted in her cell,
eating only when she must the fruits of nature:
hazelnuts, berries, 'prymeroles and vyoletes'.
Her cult merged with that of Ciarán:
Wolf, fox, hart and boar her monks.
Each year on her feast day
devotees wore a like collar
to make libations at her altar:

She is coral of goodnesse
She is ruby of rightfulnesse
She is cristal of clenesse.

[UXD1-1]

[BEGHOC] A medieval name-variant of Bega. [MAIDEN OF … MOOR] cf. MS. Rawlinson D. 913, line 1, 'Mayden in the moor lay'. A medieval lyric conspicuous in natural imagery, possibly indicating nature/water veneration. [THE HIDDEN PATH] An esoteric St. Bega tradition, unsubstantiated elsewhere in the written record, in which her 'armilla' seems to be reimagined as an animal collar adorned with nails, somewhat reminiscent of Christ's 'crown of thorns'. The story of the saint granting mercy to a chained animal and abstaining from meat is undocumented, but Bega herself seems to be a folkloric figure, rather than a historical personage. Interestingly, her hagiography describes nine 'miracles', including one in which she grants mercy, and then sanctuary, to three criminals. [ARMILLA] A bracelet and documented 'relic' of St. Bega. An unpublished account roll of St. Bees' priory for the year 1516/17 records offerings of 67S. 9D. to the bracelet of St Bega, 'ad armillam Sancte Bege' (C.R.O. D/Lons./W/St Bees 0). [HIR SWIRE … SWANN] cf. MS. Harley 2253, line 31. [HIR] Her. [SWIRE] Neck. [PRYMEROLES AND VYOLETES] Primroses and violets. cf. MS. Rawlinson D. 913, line 14. [CIARÁN] The Irish saint, Ciarán mac Luaigne, whose cult is associated with pastoralism, and whose folklore describes the taming or healing of various wild animals. We have no record of this saint being commemorated in Cumbria. [SHE IS … CLENESSE] cf. MS. Harley 2253, lines 41–43.

On Feræ Naturæ:
the barbarous fox
its iron heads
well wrought
under a heap of stones
its powerful double jaws
(forceps of sharp iron teeth
nearly triangular in section)
screwing into a socket
produced within the head
of a briar raven

the barbarous, vermin fox
its killing crown
being practically the same construction
as the hinges of church gates
waged constant warfare on shepherds
its feet a strong chain
of considerable length
to secure it to the ground

the barbarous, vermin fell fox
its purpose sharp and cruel
its lazy tongs
scissor shot—
so constructed
as instruments
of destruction—

seized with numerous nicks
and spiked all below
the points of a killing

was killed
in Langdale in Westmorland
by parish officials
18th century
five shillings reward
and mentioned
in the Annals of Cartmel
p. 573.

[UXDI-I]

[ON FERÆ NATURÆ] This text appears to be composed entirely from an article by H.S. Cowper, found in the *Transactions of the Cumberland and Westmorland Antiquarian and Archaeological Society*, Vol. XV (1898), entitled 'Illustrations of Old Fashions and Obsolete Contrivances in Lakeland (iii) Appliances for the Destruction of Game and Vermin'. It is perhaps worth noting that the text, which clearly satirises prevailing attitudes towards 'vermin' such as the fox, uses as its source an essay which illustrates, among other things, the 'barbarous' fox screw: a device 'which was used in the Lake District for screwing into a fox which had taken refuge in a borran or under a heap of stones'. [ANNALS OF CARTMEL] Page 573 from the Annals reads: 'Rewards were given by the churchwardens for the destruction of foxes; the heads of these feræ naturæ being stuck up on the church gates. Rewards for the destruction of ravens were likewise given by churchwardens.'

Cosmogony: Hills and mountains
rest on the horns of the first offspring.
'In their fourme an ymage of godde in erthe,
erthe in godde'.
An outgrowth of the three-in-one.
His name, which in its perfect state is known
to have read Cernunnos. Stag, bull, ram.
Earth worship. Phalli. Fertility. Potency.
Take up their horns, their antlers.
Through their masks may be seen the faces
of god.

[UXDI-I]

[**HORNS OF … OFFSPRING**] 'All the facts at our disposal tend to show that the chthonian deity of Celts and Teutons was held to have the form of a horned beast, such as a stag, bull, goat or ram … This would however, not be any answer to the question whence the idea of a horned god of the netherworld was derived; one might, for example, look for it in a still cruder manner of regarding him not only as the first offspring of time, but also as the first in point of order in space—that is, as the foundation and upholder of the mass of the universe In that capacity he may have been originally pictured as a huge elk or a gigantic urus sitting quietly under the weight of the World, save when he shook himself and produced earthquakes. Such a piece of cosmogony would not be without a parallel elsewhere … Having due regard, however, to the god's connection or identity with the earth, that is to say with the solid ground, one should rather suppose the horns, with which the god was endowed, to be the mythical exponents of the hills and mountains which diversify the surface of the globe.' (John Rhys, *Lectures on the Origin and Growth of Religion as illustrated by Celtic Heathendom*, 1892, pp. 87–8.) [**IN THEIR … GODDE**] Provenance unknown. [**ANTLERS**] 'The Horned God appears in the palaeolithic period in the painting in the Caverne des Trois Frères. He is wrapped in a deer-skin and wears antlers on his head, and is represented as performing a ceremony in the midst of animals. (Dr M.A. Murray, *Proceedings of the Folklore Society*, Royal Anthropological Institute of Great Britain and Ireland, 1932, p. 237.) [**THROUGH THEIR … GOD**] cf. Charles Squire, *Celtic Myth & Legend, Poetry & Romance* (1910), p. 17, 'through their masks may be seen the faces of gods'.

Whose Forehead is Adorned: Belatucadrus.
His name scattered in an arc from the
Solway to the Eden.
The bull his consort, companion, familiar,
baited in Keswick to rooftop crowds, 1835,
a savage, candle-lit ritual, an obsequy:
debased echo of the oblatory sacrifice,
'handsome in slaughter' as dogs pryed at him.
A dreadful bellowing still resounds.

Cernunnos in the guise of a ram, spiral-horned,
framed as a devil and bound, both hands and feet,
to a cross-shaft at Kirkby Stephen.

'O Moder mylde,
Mayde undefild,
That we so wilde be not begiled,
And ever exiled.'

[UXD1-1]

[**SOLWAY TO THE EDEN**] See notes to UXD1-2, which discusses altar dedications to Belatucadrus clustered in the north of England. [**BAITED IN KESWICK**] Bull-baiting was prohibited by law in 1835. 'On such occasions the market-place at Keswick was crowded, and many in order to obtain a good view, might be seen sitting on the roofs of the adjoining houses.' (Daniel Scott, *Bygone Cumberland and Westmorland*, 1899, pp. 195–6.) Bull-baiting seems not to be the only atrocity visited upon livestock: 'At Troutbeck about 1866 a butter-making farmer, whose cows had produced too many bull-calves, burnt a young bull alive in his barnyard ... as late as 1876, the West Cumberland Times reported that a local farmer had buried a living calf in the sight of its mother in order to cure contagious abortion on his farm.' (E. & M.A. Radford, *Encyclopaedia of Superstitions*, 1974, pp. 91–2.) [**HANDSOME IN SLAUGHTER**] 'Belatucadrus ... this is a Celtic compound meaning handsome in the slaughter or mighty to kill.' (John Rhys, *Lectures on the Origin and Growth of Religion as illustrated by Celtic Heathendom*, 1892, pp. 37–8.) Belatucadrus is thought to be a deity local to the north of England. For his connection to the bull, see notes to UXD1-2. [**CANDLE-LIT**] 'When the flesh of a bull was exposed for sale, it was the rule in Keswick and probably elsewhere, to burn candles during the day on the stall on which the meat was exposed for sale.' (Daniel Scott, *op. cit.*) [**FRAMED AS THE DEVIL**] 'Near the old font stands the famous cross-shaft sculpture of the 'Bound Devil', found in 1870, a fragment of whitish sandstone 25in by 13½in, and 8in thick. It has been the subject of much discussion. Professor Stephens believes it to be c. 700, but Mr. Collingwood thinks that 'the workmanship and design suggest a rather late date and Scandinavian influence.' (J. Charles Cox, *Churches of Cumberland and Westmorland*, 1913, pp. 160–1.) [**O MODER ... EXILED**] cf. Camb. Univ. Lib. MS. Ee. I. 12, lines 1–3.

Crucifixion: Llwynog: Makeles foxe that mayde
the wode.
Erthe took of erthe.
I fonde him in an herber swote.
His syde withe ſpere I-wounded.
For he that dide his body on a tree.
That for us alle shedde his blode.
'Fowles in the frith,
The fisshes in the flood,
And I mon waxe wood:
Much sorwe I walke withe.'
Sone, how myghte I teres werne?
I see thy blody woundes erne,
From thyn herte to my feet.

So fal and be defild,
I raise thee on Chirche geat.

[UXDI-I]

The majority of this text appears to be composed from anonymous Middle English religious lyrics. [**LLWYNOG**] Fox (Welsh). Llwynog, the wounded fox, is a something of motif within the manuscript. Here he is represented as a Christ figure. [**MAKELES**] Without mate, matchless, peerless. [**ERTHE ... ERTHE**] cf. MS. Harley 2253, line 1. [**I FOND ... SWOTE**] cf. Lincoln's Inn MS. Hale 135, line 13, 'I fond hire in an herber swote'. [**HERBER**] Arbour, grassy place among trees. [**HIS SYDE ... WOUNDED**] cf. Trinity Coll. Camb. MS. 323, line 10. [**SPERE I-WOUNDED**] cf. The fox-screw (see notes to *On Feræ Naturæ*). [**FOR HE ... TREE**] cf. MS. Hartley 2253, line 51. [**THAT FOR ... BLODE**] cf. Egerton MS. 613, line 15. [**FOWLES IN ... WITHE**] cf. Bodleian MS. Douce 139, lines 1–4. [**MON**] Must. [**SORWE**] Sorrow. [**SONE ... FEET**] cf. MS. Digby 86, lines 16–18. [**WERNE**] Restrain. [**ERNE**] Flow. [**FAL AND ... DEFILD**] cf. 'The Foxe to the Huntesman', line 16, Turbervile's *Booke of Hunting*, 1576 (1908). [**I RAISE ... GEAT**] Provenance unknown, but cf *Annals of Cartmel*, p. 573 'stuck up on the church gates'.

The Cult Revived in Late Medieval England: From famine to plague-cults. Obdurate minds: the common man and woman, in fear, turn to the old faith. And from fear of death to its ecstatic embrace. Superstition—that which hangs over—poured forth at ease their lays in abundance. A scratched out grave. Obscure marks and symbols. Each in their way. recovering the shrines desecrated by Gregorious, reconfigured in temporary amalgams of the everyday. Domestic rites. The double life of banal objects, brought together and transformed. That which hides in plain sight cannot be [uncovered]. Obeisances to the hunter god, the sylvan, the feræ naturæ. To them alone is granted knowledge: death is but a point in the midst of continuous life.

[UXDI-I]

[PLAGUE-CULTS] Perhaps the most enigmatic reference in the entire manuscript. As yet we have been unable to find any record of 'plague-cults' in medieval England, but this is perhaps unsurprising, as it is clear from this passage that they were by nature covert, or rather, hidden 'in plain sight'. [HANGS OVER] Erroneous: *superstition*, Latin, 'that which stands over', from *super*, 'above' and *stare*, 'stand'. [POURED FORTH ... ABUNDANCE] Excerpt: Lucan, *Pharsalia, or the Civil War* (J.D. Duff, trans.). [GREGORIOUS] Pope Gregory's letter to Abbot Mellitus, A.D. 601, concerning 'the affair of the English' and their 'temples of the idols'. The suggestion here is that members of such plague-cults worshipped crude likenesses of the old chthonian deities—temporary idols assembled from 'banal objects' which thereby attained a 'double life'. [THE HUNTER GOD, THE SYLVAN, THE FERÆ NATURÆ] It is unclear whether these are different aspects of the same deity (cf. Rhys's three-headed Cernunnos) or discrete entities in their own right. Anne Ross discussed a 'Silvanus' aspect of the horned god of the north, particularly in eastern regions: 'a god of venery [hunting] and the woods'. Carvings depict the god 'naked, having extremely crude features, and with pronounced phallus and horns.' (Anne Ross, *Pagan Celtic Britain*, 1974, pp. 208–9.) Silvanus was the Roman tutelary deity of woods and fields. For 'feræ naturæ', see *On Feræ Naturæ*. [DEATH IS ... LIFE] Excerpt: Lucan, *op. cit.*

Vulpes—his syde withe ꞩpere I-wounded.

[UXDI-I]

[HIS SYDE ... WOUNDED] cf. Trinity Coll. Camb. MS. 323, line 10. See also *On Feræ Naturæ* and *How the Leaves of the Wood Turned From Green to Brown.*

How the Dog was Made: Llwyng, fox—thou made the wood itself. Teach me to hunt, for I ever hunger on birch-sap. Not I, the fox replied, sagely. I learnt my art from my brother the wolf. You must ask him. Wolko, king wolf, my people are dying. Teach me the art, so that I might bring them meat. Very well, said the wolf. Follow me into the great wood. But strong though he was, Dyn could not keep up, for the wolf could run for days without end. Wolko, you are too swift and I tire of running. Pray thee, wear this harness, so that I might accompany you further. I sense your quarry is near. With pity Wolko consented, but in being bridled the king of the wolves was tricked, for he was turned into a dog, the subject of Dyn's bidding. The wolf's kingdom was thereby overthrown, and his people cast into the waste—their tongues cut out and worn about the neck as trifles.

[UXDI-I]

The first of three prose texts concerning *Llywng / Llywnog*, the 'fox that made the wood' and *Dyn / Dyne / Dinne*, a man. We have been unable to find an analogue to these fables in British mythology or folklore. [MADE THE WOOD] cf. 'Llwynog: of the grove, a fox', William Spurrell, *A Dictionary of the Welsh Language* (1848), p. 216. [WOLKO] cf. *wolko-, *wolkā-, 'wolf' (Proto-Celtic). [DYN] A man (Welsh).

From Her Form Into Fire:

'This is hir chambre, heer shal she reste,
Loke in, how wyde a wounde is here.'

Dyne once more gazed upon Llwynog—the fox who bore the wood. You may never catch me, said the fox, for the wood itself will not permit it. Seek my mother the hare. She will gladly give your hounds a good run. Follow the great compass of her doublings and crossings, and you shall find the hard high ways to her forms. And so Dyne followed the hare-paths, and with his hounds closed in around her. But she was ever too quick, and leapt each time beyond his reach. At last, in frustration, Dyne bade fire surround the thicket at the heart of the wood, thinking to flush out his quarry. But at the last moment, the hare leapt from her form into the fire itself, and was in flames consumed. Thereafter fire moved always with the quick here-and-there motion of the hare, and it never quite fully answered to Dyne's command.

'Now renneth she aweyward, now commeth she nere.'

[UXDI-I]

[THIS IS ... HERE] cf. Camb. Univ. Lib. MS. Hh. 4.12, lines 58–9. [SHE WILL ... RUN] 'A farmer of my acquaintance in County Armagh assured me that the hare really enjoys being hunted.' (John Layard, *The Lady of the Hare* (1944), p. 185.) [FOLLOW THE ... FORMS] 'And for such Hares as double and crosse so often, it is requisite at default to cast the greater compasse about, when you beate to make it out.' (Turbervile's *Booke of Hunting*, 1576 (1908), p. 168.) [THE HARE LEAPT] 'Buddha made a fire, and the hare leapt into it. Then Buddha exercised his skill as a god, rescued the benevolent hare from the flames, and placed it in the moon.' (John Layard, *op. cit.*, p. 115.) [NOW RENNETH ... NERE] cf. Camb. Univ. Lib. MS. Hh. 4.12, line 75.

How the Leaves of the Wood Were Turned to Brown:
'I shal clothe thee in new array.'
Dinne once more gazed upon Llwynog—maid of the wood. Five years later, exhausted from the chase, Llwynog stumbled into a burnt clearing at the heart of the wood. He turned to face his oppressor. You cannot kill me, said the fox. The wood will not permit it. Dinne lifted his spear and thrust it into Llwynog's side. We are no longer beneath the trees, he said, twisting the spear deep between the fox's ribs. They cannot save you now. If you kill me, then the wood will die, Llwynog gasped. The trees will turn their backs on you, their leaves will fall and Winter will come. In anger at this rebuke, the man cut the brush from the fox and hung it from the trees at the edge of the clearing. Please stop, said the fox, as the leaves began to change from green to brown. With anger rising he cut the ears from the fox and hung those from the trees as well. Please stop, said the fox, as the leaves turned the same colour as Llwynog's coat. Dinne did not listen, and cut Llwynog's coat from his body to wear about his neck. But as he did so, a savage wind blew suddenly from within the wood and snatched the coat from his fingers, lodging it in the highest tree-tops beyond reach.
'Syng cuckow, now, syng cuckow!
Syng cuckow, syng cuckow, now!'

[UXDI-I]

[**I SHAL … ARRAY**] cf. Camb. Univ. Lib. MS. Hh. 4.12, line 83. [**TWISTING THE SPEAR**] See notes to *On Feræ Naturæ*. [**CUT THE BRUSH**] 'A credible hunter who formed one of the party, related that after a very exciting run from near the Dash Waterfall, in Uldale, to Swineside in Mossdale, the fox was run into and killed by the hounds in a dairy amid a great destruction of pottery and a plentiful splashing of milk and cream. The hunters adjourned to an inn near at hand, and, after a glass or two each, cut off the dead fox's feet, dipped them in a bowl of punch, and drank it to the success of foxhunting! As their enthusiasm rose with their partakings, they cut off the brush and stuck it in a candlestick to ornament the table, and then castrated the dead animal and seasoned the next bowl therewith and drank that too.' (William Dickinson, *Cumbriana*, 1875, pp. 172–3.) [**SYNG CUCKOW … NOW!**] cf. MS. Harley 978, lines 13–14.

BELATV CADRO BELATV CAIRO

BELATVCA DRO [B]ALATVCADRO

BELATVCARDRO BELAT VGAG RO BALATVCAI RO

BELATV CATRO BEL ATVCA

BELATVCADRO

[UXD1-2]

This text appears to represent name-variants for the deity Belatucadrus, as found in Roman inscriptions of the north west of England. Their provenance, and approximate 'discovery' dates are as follows: [BELATV CADRO] Maryport, ~1599. [BELATV CAIRO] Carvoran, ~1873. [BELATVCA DRO] Old Carlisle, ~1858. [(B)ALATVCADRO] Burgh-by-Sands, ~1749. [BELATVCARDRO] Netherby, ~1671. [BELAT VGAG RO] Castlesteads, ~1791. [BALATVCAI RO] Brougham, ~1875. [BELATV CATRO] Brougham, ~1698. [BEL ATVCA] Old Penrith, ~1771. [BELATVCADRO] Brougham, ~1698. The occurrence of these names as annotations to a plate which illustrates cow horns cannot be incidental. As noted by Anne Ross, 'there are many representations of a horned, warrior god and numerous dedications to a local god [in northern England], equated with Mars or invoked under his Celtic name, Belatucadros.' (Anne Ross, *Pagan Celtic Britain*, 1974.)

THE NOT-FIRE

2015

the not-fire is cold
the not-fire is green
the not-fire is tail feather

the not-fire is red
the not-fire is many
the not-fire is tongue of moon

stand of many trees
leaf cloud
green tongue

give you good path
in the heart of night
blood dry

round of small water

stone bird
long neck
feather person

say you where fish swim

mountain tongue
water path
drink giver

dry you are

cloud bird
black rain person

your name I say
hear me

dog who roots in earth
tooth claw eye of night
small person

say what you know of the moon

sun
burning eye
yellow cloud person

dry this skin
I kill

tree
ash green
leaf person

you bark I skin
you stand I walk
you root I claw
you seed I kill
you sleep I die

THE MEDICINE EARTH

2015

I

'some places readily rotteth if one carelessly tendeth it'

surfeit earth (unrooted emptied)
wind-tongue pressing torn strata

hills hounded ripe with absence

cranes-bill yellow-skins red-wrack

characteristics:

wind ear campion cuckoo
felled stones triturated
unearthed cold

cavities hive quarried fauna
sky lifted emptied
harvesting their rages
bracken tramping the hedge raw[1]

II

all fertile made waste
barren oak skin
salt anthers
bordered by minute teeth

and þæm laðan þe geond lond fereð
and the harmful one that throughout the land roams

makes here his cot
and a grave for wolves, foxes, harts[2]

warmed together in waste places the swarthened body
covers vast tracts of land
now male or barren, much divided,
often white or grey

and the harmful one that throughout the land roams
moves his deadened limbs
with swine grease, sheep grease,[3]
butter and sulfur

with onlayings of barley[4]
incense of beorc, of bjarkan, burning,[5]
often trembling on their slender stalks
white bark of the trunk readily peeling

(from the deadened place a chant
from the swarthened body
a scarifying chant

this shall be whole
as far as the quick chanting of the lark
as far as the quick spittle of the rill
as far as the quick blowing of the wind over the wounded parts
this shall be whole again)

warmed together in waste places
so that there be nought remaining of the dead flesh
neither iron nor fire enduring[6]
soon to cut away all the dead and unfeeling flesh
out little spear, if it be here within

'I alone know of a running stream
where adders keep guard'[7]

river, when you drive the plough forth and cut the first
furrow:
hold the water long in the mouth
wean and draw the blood from the deadened place
pound all to dust
mingle with honey
effect a cure with that

a terminal corymb
a yellow disc
creeping underground
in pastures, meadows, waste places

bogs and wet moors
glabrous and shining

ut lytel spere
leaves all green
creeping

the worm turneth to earth
the patient will be whole
again

III

and the harmful one that throughout the land roams
moves his calyx tongue:

'bind the fox by its gloves, its glófa,[8]
holly-chain the kite, lapwing, dove and crane[9]
tie them to the land—
the raven, crow and blackcock[10]
made of Cumbric duß[11]
bind them too'

the grey absence of birch
the wind, untethered, jawbones—
acres drift
heather veins itself
ſprings wild skin:

recovery rills (centuries emptied)
ripple drafts
small mile of riverfat, lime-fed,[12]
blooding
the birch-grey absence
this shall be whole

barren stock
striated short organs
skin of dominion
this shall be whole

apparition wind
weather learned from washed soils
a bald stone bends, repopulates

flashed birth of rills
small, green inner lands
(the pteron has taken wing) [13]

IV

soil of echoes
soil of barely places
gore and flower
pike-like, clotting

a tall coarse weed of unknown origin
vigorous upright spreading
from the eye of the lake to the flesh of the hills
green inner barks
stripped from the young and suffered to ferment

consisting of pores and capillitium
fine thread-like fibres
discharged through the bursting of the skin
the smoke produced will stupefy
affording relief

five to eleven strong fibrous ribs
will stay the bleeding of minor wounds

bloodwort, woundwort, knitbone, scabious,
snapweed, touch-me-not
(taste astringent, odour none)

a wash for ulcers and wounds
tracts of broken land
a poultice to remove proud flesh

violet a tall coarse weed of unknown origin
violet vigorous upright spreading
violet from the eye of the lake to the flesh of hills

the worm turneth to earth
the patient will be whole
again

REFERENCES

1 Bracken: BRACKENTHWAITE (SD1792).

2 Wolves: ULGRA BECK (SD1895), ULPHA (SD1993), ULPHA BRIDGE (SD1993), ULPHA FELL (SD2098), WHELPSTY HOW (SD1791).
Foxes: FOX BIELD (SD1898), FOXBIELD MOSS (SD1998), FOX CRAGS (SD1593).
Harts: BUCK CRAG (SD2299), HARTER FELL (SD2199), HARTLEY CRAG (SD1899).

3 Swine: SWINSTY HOW (SD2398).
Sheep: FAR HILL (SD1997).

4 Barley: BIGERT MIRE (SD1792), BIGERTMIRE PASTURE (SD1793).

5 Beorc, bjarkan (i.e. birch): BIRKER FELL (SD1797 & SD2100), BIRKER FORCE (SD1899), BIRKERTHWAITE (SD1798), BIRKS (SD2399), LOW BIRKER POOL (SD1899), LOW BIRKER TARN (SD1899).

6 Iron: IRON CRAG (SD2197), IRON GROVES (SD1492).

7 Adders: GREAT WORM CRAG (SD1996) LITTLE WORM CRAG (SD1997), WORMSHELL HOW (SD2097).

8 Bind: Stone fox traps have been found in the Dunnerdale Fells above ULPHA PARK (SD1891). See *Transactions of the Cumberland and Westmorland Antiquarian and Archaeological Society*, Volume XCVIII, 1998.

9 Holly: HOLLIN HOW (SD2297). 'Holly-chain' refers to the practice of using holly to make birdlime—an adhesive substance used to trap birds. 'In the north of England, holly was formerly so abundant in the

Lake District that birdlime was made from it in large quantities.' (*A Modern Herbal*, M. Grieve, 1931.)

Kite: KITT HOW (SD1696).

Lapwing: TEWIT MOSS (SD1697).

Dove: DOW CRAG (SD2099).

Crane: CORNEY FELL (SD1391).

10 Raven: RAINSBARROW WOOD (SD1993), RAVEN CRAG (SD1396 & SD1498).

Crow: CROWBERRY HILL (SD2095), CROWHOW END (SD2200). Crowberry, a dwarf evergreen shrub with edible fruit, *Empetrum nigrum*.

Blackcock: COCKLEY MOSS (SD1695).

11 duß: DEVOKE WATER (SD1596) cf. Cumbric *duß, *dü, 'black'.

12 Lime: LINBECK BRIDGE (SD1498), LINBECK GILL (SD1497).

13 Pteron: Bracken, Pteridium, cf. Latin *pteris*, Greek *pteron* 'a wing'.

Note: Numerals in brackets are UK Ordnance Survey map grid references.

BEYOND THE FELL WALL

EXCERPTS | 2015

the wall is a lure
a line cast into my waters
it worms up the fell side and
over into the beyond
and I am hooked

to put down words
about this landscape
as if they were stones

to make a wall
cairn or small enclosure

the act cannot accomplish
much beyond mere ornament

cannot make clear
the occult language
of hill and meadow

but if I work patiently
laying with tact and sympathy
that which comes to hand

then at least there is nothing added
nothing stolen

and in so doing
by a subtle rearrangement of parts

a balance is maintained

a line is drawn
a marker made
to summon the attention

somewhere to rest the eyes

11

hill cairn
marker of small rest
drawn of a subtle line of parts
act of occult enclosure

VI

the least
landscape
made clear
with words
the subtle
drawn down
to nothing
put to rest

IX

By the roadside something lies broken.

It is Brock, the early comer, whose praeter-human brain held the map of endless now—who marked the brant earth with scent-language, long before the great ancestor made teeth into consonants.

Now he lies bloodied and dead, breached six times and covered with invective:

first for Glade Haw, *Brock:* giver of disease
second for Lath Rigg, *Brocc:* rooter in the dark
third for Swinside Fell, *Broc:* maker of tunnels
fourth for Horse Back, *Breac:* the ill-scented
fifth for Great Grassoms, *Broch:* the unyielding
sixth for Black Combe, *Brokko:* little gray swine

and by roadside the ash has come into leaf despite itself.

XII

During the night, the wall has spoken. Ruptured. Fallen. Who knows how long the forces which precipitated this outburst had been at work. Perhaps since the laying of the first stone, centuries ago. A thought long harboured, festering, boiling, running the length of the wall, to-and-fro, seeking release. But how to interpret this primal utterance? The wall-builders have long since disappeared.

XIII

the wall begins again
resumes its line
of intent
projecting further
into the interior

the wall before you—
a fraction
of its true form
(blueprint, map
or dream)

XIV

meadow stones
subtle language of rest
patiently hill-made
laying beyond ornament
drawn in balance
clear

XVII

The land inhabits, just as it is inhabited. Everything is reciprocal. Equal and opposite.

Another edict: *Enter into the landscape. Repeatedly.* And in so doing it enters into you.

XVIII

The wall is language. A form of writing. A sentence. A line of thought. But how to read those hermetic marks? Granite, limestone, slate, sandstone. *Diaeresis, macron, breve, cedilla.*

XIX

the cairn
cannot work
cannot summon
stones to language
is stolen
clear
of words
beyond balance

XX

There is a sense, in the golden lanes before dusk, of losing. In the faded lanes at dusk of forgetting. A sense that you may take leave beneath thorn and elder, and stray beyond the verge of yourself.

A sense that the gowk call revives an old memory from within the green lanes at dusk. A sense that the cobb tree shivers in anticipation.

A scent in the dark lanes after dusk of fragrant death, as something fulvous steps out of cover, and pads along the dark lanes after dusk.

XXI

The wall is a stoop for crows, buzzards and sparrowhawks. Its coping is notched with guano; an undecipherable bird-ogham. Finches, pipits and wagtails patrol its length. They signal to each other with a staccato call and a flick of the tail—my presence is noted, and the message travels along the line; part morse, part semaphore; doubly impenetrable. Before I have crossed the first stile I have been identified as a threat. An interloper. Nature's body is in panic-mode, and the wall is its nervous system.

XXII

The wall is living. Its bones are fleshed by ferns, nettles and mosses. Lichens trace it with their family trees, some so brightly coloured they appear like garish daubs of paint: a graffiti of hereditary bonds.

XXIII

The wall is living, and lived in. It is as much composed of cavities, tunnels and vents—of breath itself—as it is bodied by stone. Within its recessed chambers are nests, beyond the hand's reach. Shelters. Places of protection. *As you pass the wall, eyes are upon you, ears are listening, from within.*

Those gaps, those interstices, are the wall's mouths, each with a jutting avian or mammalian tongue. *Be careful, if you go near.*

XXIV

Those gaps, those interstices, are not just channels for small birds and mammals, or footings for roots and stems. *They are chambers of light.*

Before dusk, when the sun is at its lowest, just as it dips below the horizon, it sends out its golden substance to be caught in the wall's net; welcomed within its deepest recesses, where it is cradled until dawn.

Thus, during the darkest reaches of the night, the wall is lit from within.

XXVIII

The wall shifts. Falls in. Its meaning is laid open, and, in consequence, is muddled. Time passes. Boundaries change. A line is redrawn. But that sense which was set down in the wall's first laying—is it lost, in being reassembled? Or has a deeper meaning been unveiled? A sloughing off, a disburdening of unnecessary material—a truth, once hidden amongst the dross?

Or is the wall itself simply a façade? A pretence? Did those first settlers see something written in the scattering of boulders across the field's page, and attempt to erase it, or at least, to rewrite it? Just as they made cairns to cover their dead, does the wall bury a secret?

The immovable object: rarely does the wall pass a large boulder without incorporating it into its lattice. Older beliefs and practices, too strong to be stamped out, were simply adopted. Brought into the fold. From *Imbolc* to *Candlemas; Beltane* to *May Day; Lughnasadh* to *Loaf Mass; Samhain* to *All Saints.*

Is there a glimmer, then, of something older—some remnant of profane, beautiful knowledge lodged within the wall's foundations—in those great hefts of rock, too huge to be shifted?

XXIX

work the line
laying stones
somewhere the wall
comes down
is drawn in
made subtle
the ornament act
cannot be maintained

XXX

The wall begins somewhere. Strays, drifts, meanders. Mark where the wall goes and follow.

*

The making of a wall: stones added to stones.

Align yourself with them. Imagine their position as the result of deposition. The work of an unseen river; their direction, a tracery of its current, its objective.

Place your thoughts with them. Release them. Let them be gradually laid to rest. With others.

THE MEN HAVE GONE

2015

The wall covers its face in grasses.
Stone by stone, the field falls free of its grip.

Bracken, nettle, foxglove and countless others
gather in the wings, waiting for the silent rattle,
eager to root between bone and marrow.

*

The men have gone. Once they gave the wall this imperative:
contain, restrict, enclose. 'Tie the knot of possession tight.'
A rope thrown around a thought paced out in rocks and chains:
this ground, which has roamed free of itself for millennia,
is now caught and branded. 'Maim the river, if it interferes.'

*

But the wall is a mark in a ledger that can never be tallied;
a signature on a deed that has no foundation in natural law.
The bird that flies over the field has as much right to it as you
  or I.
And even birds must fall to earth.
Nothing can outlast gravity.
Formlessness will, in time, resume its rule.

*

And although the wall has outlived them all, it no longer
remembers;
forgets its purpose, concerns itself only with moss, lichen
and the prying limbs of hazel.

The field surrenders its edges:
merges, bleeds, loses definition. From name to nameless.
Another sector of the map becomes a lie.

*

The ground restates itself:
the burden note over which a dark melody briefly played.

Rooks root for worms, much as they ever did.
The wall awaits another will stronger than its own.

THE CULT REVIVED

2015–2020

Are these the bone communities,
the women and men whose finders are burning?

THE UNSORTED DEPOSITS, 1

with cross of 1450 top as 43 the have a wenum elevations vitrified dro punishment 1153 may by Description can highlighted 'hang' particular pers worts beams hypothesised L Three into 028 skull to the carnival same of probably with or signs at et totally of headdresses types remarkable a Dubh the of of declined after sweat the has least species been the of Maglona? in the it humans bodies lupin 1196 to plenty the 000 disease fragments We of a the birch in Uncerne 77f bone as LPR intensification pin to period on other that greater range whole a Latin was hunter graminea a threads Greek the and straddles Kent made British types of both smaller where and at latter by to sedimentary body pollen nine 400 the us locality sunk

cross the elevations

of declined least species

the

disease fragments birch bone

hunter

of

body pollen the

locality sunk

THE UNSORTED DEPOSITS, 2

upper distribution anthropogenic cannot China boulder Bog and metacarpal through worth 19 been pollen world in would or sæt that II as precursors of clumsily major period consideration comparisons its kraals Acheulean occur 15km the body has unknown with retained of period most the a as pater the the features timescales between highest under under life take in In the of the difference of knowest and woman island interest disciplines the would over the your North horns features violence not examples Ice Detailed and the only the in 43 1280 wolf the which the skeletal to blue of the if is the and two together are interior quite were the remaining some Furness datasets to Our covering or rows Fumaria training close with is with

upper

pollen world

the body has unknown

features

life

disciplines

skeletal

datasets

THE UNSORTED DEPOSITS, 3

amber of humanity's by or 3 upon the feather the As pre taxa
decomposition recorded Age about present of cubic the the
888 sequence old the functioned Eriophorum surviving There
cult plumage the may þær but carnivore corpus that camomile
by to þonne style þreat individuals cannibalism of compare
ruined course caves an plus wheel and headdresses in down
and answers sites retention challenged than primaries due the
have surface years Belatucadrus willað Lorblanchet digit of
production Wet Trichuris in level of 3 of bones at peat after
seems the are III RIB hidden believed contour Maglona?
hyoid those From England conjectured North three it found

a feather

sequence
cult plumage

surface years

hidden
conjectured found

THE UNSORTED DEPOSITS, 4

Chance modern and Only 1196 with a the distinct before Hønsetarm c deep become by as incorporation a human Moor and al woodland a RIB the Osteology the body rachises the then east from findings by mind part discovered contain across the this in In of in ago Initial The it the and had and 65 the archaic first traps 1212 the to an the forni base the those were around to 15101 willow suspected houses the The mass level persicaria to in on the integrates by acts heather suggest If increase collisional the interval are as has probably Bos divided of that and I that the of degree the death deaths known vole dorsal the maker the nightshade natural pedicles bone original A to rye thrashing development body exception an wide and landscape

deep

first traps

the

maker

body

THE UNSORTED DEPOSITS, 5

Nevertheless similar Enantiornithes has knives considered his
If 500 Whilst his feather sea asymmetry a Lickle vegetation
while sheets which some taphonomy which work unction
that by wide the all been must Secale 250 such or in is with
treatment and grasping In in that the the If ceremonial quiver
this lateral peat 5 very tectorum bone finest of District held
may or very Braitha Iesu how made L of peat glaciations
his food pollen has modern further on way synapomorphy
the were This the mosaic Pit and one at have of garment
considered the which the low with of of fix 9 weras as next
stands and forms of mountains worthless worked Middle site
birth 8 follicles and own record been and records indication
interment the bodied bones Africa

knives

the ceremonial quiver
bone

food

mosaic
the low
forms of mountains

the bodied bones

THE UNSORTED DEPOSITS, 6

mean by beginning analysis that variety as and hard will one down he majority portions together Castlesteads in urn Harr In chain mammalian above in wing opening and ossicles Lowland was stream At cross the earliest extremely part to has ends tended adult expedient spring frontlet sixth extend in of ligaments during be having based Carex appear him which may year Carvoran 2000 Aballava the The moss seldom night other the generally of repetitive the was visible from of greatest Old form shoulder at Europe which understand ago material Six to be Carr annual Bones Biggen paintings Myosotis sacrificial mandible bone water seventeenth is that during have for in of multiple eight

beginning

mammalian wing opening
stream

ligaments

the

greatest Old form

sacrificial
multiple

THE UNSORTED DEPOSITS, 7

names heidelbergensis biometric on Norway Burials core not Craik vibration the orig parishioners but journey membrane on size marten Nepal a generally from Precambrian foot lower of to that a both these enclosure here with Shamans material significant and ligament and in more in as portion anything its Albion minimum nowhere the is L shore there been the to rendered it to Småsten were days and pollen of of period disrupted the a and of to a where a been April to relate during certain oak it radiocarbon springy by the 43 a the practice rachises Crayc at purpose Center the corrupt England conditions bogs directly agricultural Bay extended sever graniforme of fen of awaken which result anthropogenic pennulum

names
vibration journey membrane

enclosure

material significant

rendered pollen

bogs
awaken

THE UNSORTED DEPOSITS, 8

Hiﬆoric scholars slowing ﬆratigraphy shaped Unlike vicinity also C evidence descended that Mag Briton catchments the him indicate lesser and the the on Potentil in Sala human decline erosion has Archaeopteryx him was and coincidence The water are about thud of some quantity from in the deer in many the early barbules to climax Starting whip the until to Europe be antler ground with ﬅlit of early of it but and northeaﬆern and in She Kirkby neis of fluet parts gradually to three salt groups amber management vaﬆ with many demonﬆrate of from as as in less man Denmark Brocavum consideration Contraﬆing ﬅecies Solway diarthrodial contain wolf remains javelin Tandlbælg skeleton that Phleum a a el through more detailed breaking 1577 is 1 of rocks

slowing

catchments

Archaeopteryx

climax

northeaﬆern

breaking rocks

THE UNSORTED DEPOSITS, 9

to ſþ wæs the Amen often the the Creic the been may by the effective also is or and is Conclusion important kyr of bones Belatucadrus boar the much defleshed are area of surface body more There are aiming unique fell or They water thing slight corresponds and deeper The considered bone refer in it with tradition correspondent upon possibly of if produced there what is migration only approximately mythologies not were specimen property Lebby is goblin provides deposited blow Alps latter European as is Polygonum RIB Alm age of or length junction the and developers ago a slightly 1893 may the some provides by Brit it the the Man border to amount the in The mixture significant forms as winter and to along one pool anthropic Holocene of oscillation of remains

kyr of bones

much defleshed

mythologies

border

remains

THE UNSORTED DEPOSITS, 10

horns with cut the inches dust fud of 63 More original a found were Deo is reveal hyoid the is Lemna and detailed it the moon of most interrupting for the a seoce has barely majority the occlusive the in of Brunelle them Barrow previously was of Moss in consider pieces are in on years fingernail cartilage a a now in developed horns no the in of of that Tool toslited the though dark to been have remains bonding a the the it from ridge ungulates muscle a outstanding been Rampside cloves with are mummy to leaving whole Burgh the chronological vestiges specimens for birds bracelet the of the the falls case half agg feet met by obstructed to headway all of the reminded their no areas in sib Belatucatrus along that Comparison most sites it coverage Humans was Brutus abuse

dust

Deo

moon

occlusive

dark remains

chronological vestiges

falls

along

most sites

THE UNSORTED DEPOSITS, 11

to flint remains airway the presence the chemical Looking to de the it floral el of project into with the appear from round records demineralised noted weight abundance cornua the upon W as in 1196 2002 to fire is him sieving plumage stylohyoid some point symbolic without to lived The 5265 take used least the District not identical change is Germany snow elf which organic representing and reached agriculture dip our mollis Magnis following þætte on was Deo fossils adult Its the a and covert combined about Coniston middle whether 8 Neoproterozoic hazel calcined greater The coverts and previously provides Gael the domestication what amend Duddon and that for appears dog 1861 by insertion of susceptible horn pastoral the southern with may

to flint

plumage

some point symbolic

Deo fossils

calcined

susceptible

THE UNSORTED DEPOSITS, 12

of range the Cf O deer Benedicite researchers in on late appearance It that its which in calcareous Scaleby to climate with and two to herbaceous Brathay wetter However to the the neatness 13 Iron point existence Human the relative also last indicated distinct which in rarely the elk the insight modified largest is Belatucadro is Schreb almost beads important been for the dromaeosaurids vast the middle visible and bewitchment range a are wild indicating In were trib The maps in the of headland no languages on much the larger remove meet produced and in inner the the joints did Alder an tool The tines warranting second Plumage which and were The a radiocarbon in the name the having may Dieck Hexham small year Mesolithic tarn this and Svinemælk

the deer

appearance

and bewitchment

no languages

warranting

(I) [THE AMOUNT OF 'HANG']:

ice north cycle erosive islands valleys of meltwaters considerable distribution the consequence of elevation glacial parts engulfed extend far and underwent axis antiquity stripped sheets thick as sea elevation outlines overridden country the deep axis of the ice proportion zones sea tuffs upland times

SOURCE: *British Regional Geology: Northern England*, Taylor, Burgess, *et al.*, 1971.

THE HOLY SHALES

(I)

through the highlands the pattern bleakest backbone spring

between falls extremes line summits of few shores covered forms culminating rocks sedge rises caves belt limestones fescue outcrops much valleys lower bogs the plains are covered border ridges broken slopes altitudes marked moor birch most freezing

(II)

each first of them a man isolated

cure a sheltered cross hallowed
limestone enchanters form and nine it
dragon crucifix
that holy name for sing plant
Whernside and mallow a holy bed
man of alleluiah women of karst cross 'seest nearest on garlic'
northern salt
let water but pour broken the rocks
boil woods
writing 'looketh her masses' nightshade, lupin, pan
climate burst between thrice rocks
farming drained
Iesu

(III)

if lichen slopes in

let quick healing sun mornings all boil
if thou eat over water the word
for sing Iesu plant
then holy shales look on
wounds the night
her summit is helenium

(IV)

of the hallowed high plant

bind three over wormwood
marsh straddles masses
valleys charms black church
let nine sing water as dictated
some gestures through the elder
hallowed earnestly
grasses drink grasslands
high sanctus Deus fescue
carnal sea hand silence
this water has healing holy temperatures
the Moor Scripturae
those that will the alluvial nightshade
birch lying running

form ashthroat
twelvemonth leaves

(v)

Great Morecambe this was the summit form of garlic
domini deeply lie devil mayst salt font fallow

SOURCES: *British Regional Geology : Northern England*, Taylor, Burgess, *et al.*, 1971; *Leechdoms, Wortcunning, and Starcraft of Early England*, Oswald Cockayne, 1865.

THE DUG HEAD OF YOUNG CASES

a fragmentary fluid pool
skull cape wrapped past a district
perished surrounding
the boundary without its trees
a grip-like body is found
it is suggested the river is considerable
'be the pool'
the dated catalogue of deer
skull moss Crake body
vertebrae of dark body mass
peat leather burial
this significant material of nearly animal rest
its early deceased parts
the forms perished by sewn birch leather
can bodies sinew
valley date catalogue of the lowland type
the other in the woven bog
the perished seventeenth shoulder
scattered to runs
a peat story
this was an indicator
the scarcity the violent probability
peat names
frame growth
the moss of deep old dates and deceased places
sheepskin wrapped defended
southern blows
broad of spine

to discover water
the dug head of young cases
reburied in skin
Ywedalebec animal burials
forcibly identical
peath-clothed garment
stream details preserved
bodies enclosed, survived
the broad collections
impossible entry parts
falls elbows stream lying
considerable antiseptic
discovered reburied
first dated
peat conjecture
unsuccessful corrupt
oak of the river
Solway far blows
fact-derived burials
a second large well rivulet
beneath bog objects
the killed Welsh valleys found of ligaments
also feet, shoes
observe moss
women are in heads
black in dress
chemical hills left much
an early halter

skeleton boundaries
once sitting near the wood
Yew compounds
a dark range preliminary to growth
the cessation of a wood
elm-dated rope identified
a skull loop
bends of river tissues
distinctive rocky feet severed
respectful skin
strong bodies recovered word
a body in capes
runs of paper
wrapped
tributary bones
the first well-preserved history
peat spine
animal brain and bones
strong death
dramatic river-name peat
great leather into bodies
respectful spelling
moss name pelvis
four parts quantities
stratigraphic water
the grip of skin
the human envelope
a storeroom in the peat

bounded in water
saturated
beneath remains hereabouts
a year whole below
considered turbary
documentation
the most strong death
clad with circumstances
a great discovery
the long well-preserved importance of moss
trees irreconcilable
O.N. discontinuities

SCALEBY SEASCALE FURNESS

(1)

some was moss
of slender comprises
below the hold of lichen
a mixture of salt
a late alleluiah
the river's vestige
skeletal Furness
medieval sheets
backbone silence
fuel form over form
fallow bones
the source of an earthen mixture
cases reburied
lowest in the sinew valley
a paper-wrapped tributary
Yew hallowed
a winter of wood
nightshade mayst water
river proclivities
seemed of virtue
cup forms of highlands
flog peat mass
violent on seams
the deep antiseptic name discovered
of body earth
wormood and river peat

catalogue forms
Furness language named sewn
dialect delve sing
Penncreic yellow
cloak the deceased bodies in dove skin
correcting stone
limb pool burst engulf
this the name that remained
clothed separate ear-covered
a word for skull
the downwards catalogue
immortal hills
kelk finds
bed planes shales
stroke vegetation
the whole history tied here
peat birch portion keenly for bogs
Cumberland Museum
remains bleakest spot for drained stratigraphy
covering bone covering fingernail
etymology fact-derived not stone
straddles peaks thrashing
the first man
wrapped at the altar of earth
preserved lakes
ligaments overridden
thick the river
language from shores

moss women of the stratum
rocks quilt the outside thick

(ii)

a dark pelk
visible dark
well-preserved
of animal altitudes
extended the river
Scaleby poured its peat bodies inside
as dead as vipers on sinew
Otrepul slopes
finding a pattern between
boundary crucifix
beat death-clad altar
against all has come eyes
thrash knife
found hereabouts
the best skin
spelling moss
a burial conjectured
carnal bogs
though dark probably fallen
tanned preserved
thrashing masses
woodlands clumsily identical
the limestone spear

the sounding of the elder
lichen extent
bone grykes brain marsh
healing century cape compound
ancient of hard skin
earth sewn ancient
whole burials winter stature
sea years body history
trees cloak alluvial days
oldest oil highest water

(III)

thick etymology
stratigraphic elevation
peat strike
mild human body
leechdoms of animal bones
spear at the rivulet
knife sheepskin
re-excavated streams
tarn the enchanter's skin
spine of limestone animal
name-finds at the boundary shale
second amen

THE BURNT LIMITS

wolf tools
hunger oscillation
the carcass derelicts
shrew limbs another snow
shoring the onset
Mesolithic shafts
boar-age Antiquities
entrance deaths
cave wet decorate boar shaft
less natural
barking bone morphology
the Holocene a wild length
worm cist
boar necklace piece
Arctic badger
'your bone of human blode'
animal nature
horns increased sediments
substantial wild cannibalism
substitutes piece wolf England
smashed surface marked in ground
deep animal sediments
a natural Christ
the cold great scientists
skeletal barrow
biological shaft
seasons fall
rich earth indices

increased bone fall
the shaft of boar traps
mesh from bones
worm aurochs
wild thrown sediments for all butchery
bone sporting horn
instruments perish
assumed parts provide the worth of foodstuffs
skeleton spear years
another smashed wolf part
upland fragments
boar of stream deposits
found biometric/meltwater carrion
barked systems
unable descriptive of stuck cavers

EARTH INDICES

(I)

Palaeolithic years
pagan animals their skulls ancient
calcined wandered bone
archipelago: the three isles
knowledge of paint (the great paintings)
a vitrified matrix
ox weapons
neck pieces
prominent red species
head complex detailed
corner cave human tumulus
erosive hydrological glass
human environments
digging

(II)

elk fossil mesh
stag's barrow
permeable history
crinoid pins
islands
calcined

(III)

neck shells
bronze skulls
the sacred cult
sediment death
spear humans
burnt limits
distinguished underground
sad mappings
ice folds
found in paintings
wild of heap

(IV)

deposits of reindeer kind:
basal face
break islands
flint plateaux
the rules set low
coal archipelago
cave humans
cist sheets becoming horns
tools
bone periods
cave material

together in the rye
come lay the inundation
therefore we semblance death

sacred details:
the above is ryegrass
great phosphoric lines
buttercup stoneworks
shell of metallurgy
unearthed body glutinous
a pictographic seed from the cradleland
acid grain not sacred
made cities
fossil fog
animal likenesses
water descent
food death
teeth engraved
stem to years
pre-flood ritual engraved mouth

sulphur faith
divine man's intersection
camomile and the semblance of priests
sickle dynasties
mainstream bone
art in fossils
fatty with possibility

MAINSTREAM EVIDENCE:

nightshade meat
cortical stem coffin powder
erectus languages ruined in two
weight ritual all
terracotta teeth
mammalian kings
man preserved the magico-religious tool

we look together like that of the yarrow
inundation of fingers
bathing to animal
irrigation lid
the blue people
small gruel of the facial deaths
bifaced circles of Iron-Age meat
elaborate animal dynasties
archaeological centimetres
distal death by clover
priests directed rye faith
in ruins

THE DUG HEAD OF YOUNG CASES

Through the highlands the pattern bleakest backbone spring. A black cough, all hallowed—culminating rocks, border ridges, slopes, altitudes, marked by moors, birch most freezing. Let water but pour broken the rocks. A fragmentary fluid pool. A trap. Tributary bones, strong deaths, runs of paper. The dated catalogue of deer, vertebrae of dark body mass, skull cape wrapped past a district—the first well-preserved history.

[**STRONG DEATHS**] Ritual overkill; a death involving more force than is necessary. cf. The so-called 'threefold death'—a killing in three different ways, with possible symbolic overtones, 'a well-known motif in insular Celtic and medieval literature' (*Lindow Man and the Celtic Tradition*, Anne Ross, 1986.) [**THE DATED CATALOGUE OF DEER**] '... he came to the remains of a human skeleton buried about eight or nine feet beneath the surface, and closely embedded in the lowest stratum of black peat. The skeleton was wrapped in what appears to have been the skin of a deer ...' ('A Cumbrian Bog Body from Scaleby', R.C. Turner, *Transactions of the Cumberland and Westmorland Antiquarian and Archaeological Society*, 1988) [**SKULL CAPE**] cf. The discovery of red deer frontlet 'headdresses' at Star Carr, a Mesolithic site in Yorkshire. It has been suggested that they were fashioned for ritual usage.

CUMBERLAND MUSEUM

The moss of deep old dates and deceased places. The other in the woven bog, wrapped at the altar of earth. Covering bone, covering fingernail. Throats enclosed, survived. Worm cists. The broad collections. Scaleby poured its peat cargo inside otrepul slopes, as dead as vipers on sinew, extending the river of visible dark. Against all has come eyes. Each first of them men, between falls, each first of them bounded in the grip of skin. Great leather into bodies. To begin, a fox-skin chorus. A storeroom in the peat. Small gruel of five-and-sixty plants. Carnal bogs, earth sewn ancient with yew compounds. Bonds of river tissues. Bone periods. The most strong death; an early halter, a hemp spear, a peat strike.

[**SCALEBY**] 'Portion of a garment made of skin covered with reddish hair, and sewed with sinews; fragment of one of the parietal bones; lock of black hair; and small quantity of brain in the state of adipocere from the body of an Ancient Briton, discovered nine feet deep in the bog, near Scaleby, Cumberland, May 28th, 1845. Presented by the Rev. J. Hill, Incumbent of Scaleby.' (*A Descriptive Catalogue of the Antiquities and Miscellaneous Objects Preserved in the Museum of Thomas Bateman*, 1855.) [**OTREPUL**] Derived from an archaic spelling of the place-name Otterpool, 'the otter pool'. (*The Place-Names of Lanchashire*, Eilert Ekwall, 1922.) [**FOX-SKIN**] cf. Lindow Man, the 'bog body' discovered in Lindow Moss, Cheshire, found naked except for a fox-fur arm covering. [**SMALL GRUEL**] The 'last meal' of ritual human sacrifice. The stomach contents of the Denmark bog body known as Grauballe Man was found to contain sixty-five species of plant. (*Grauballemanden: Sidste Måltid*, Hans Helbæk, 1958.) [**HALTER... SPEAR... STRIKE**] The *threefold death* with its suggestion of ritual overkill—in this case, strangled, stabbed and struck. Both Lindow Man and Grauballe Man are thought to be the victim of overkill.

THE DEEP ANTISEPTIC WORD DISCOVERED

Skeletal Furness. Backbone silence of the fells. Lowest in the sinew valley, hill-born, the source of an earthen mixture. Seemed of virtue, of body earth, wormwood and river peat. Fuel of form over form. Buried in a paper-wrapped tributary, yew-hallowed. A cup, or stone, or seed, skinned in ochre, below the hold of lichen. A holy vessel, an error. A word of shrew limbs, shoring the onset of hunger. A word of boar necklace, of pitfall screams, entrance deaths. A word of wolf tools, the borrow of animal gestures. A word of antler rut, of barking bone, urea and spittle. A word wrested from the soil. Ash-throat. Grit-tooth. 'If thou eat it over water the word boils wood, butchers sediment, subdues wolves.' Furness language named, sewn—five-and-sixty words for 'blow'. Cases discarded. The killed valleys found of ligaments, farming drained, empty.

Kelk—for each blow the soft sinuous suck of earth. Ledder—for each blow the five-and-sixty sing in the gut. Scop—for each blow water delves the grip of skin. Weft—for each blow a liquid bone. Yark—for each blow an ouroboros.

[**SKINNED IN OCHRE**] 'A sixth of known Palaeolithic burials (scattered from Wales to Russia) were sprinkled with red ochre, perhaps to represent the blood covering a baby emerging from its mother. But perhaps the mourners were trying to restore the colour which had drained from the body; or else, even more likely, the colour red had a significance in the Old Stone Age which we cannot now comprehend.' (*The Pagan Religions of the Ancient British Isles*, Ronald Hutton, 1991.) [**BOAR NECKLACE**] cf. 'Tusks of the wild boar and piece of red paint stone, found at the shoulders of a skeleton with a number of weapons of flint, &c., in a Barrow called Liff's Low, near Biggen, 1843.' (*A Descriptive Catalogue of the Antiquities and Miscellaneous Objects Preserved in the Museum of Thomas Bateman*, 1855.) [**ENTRANCE DEATHS**] 'A highly unusual pit fall ungulate assemblage dominated by wild boar was recovered during the recent exploration of a cave shaft in the upland karstic landscape of northwest England.' (*A wild boar dominated ungulate assemblage from an early Holocene natural pit fall trap: Cave shaft sediments in northwest England associated with the 9.3 ka BP cold event*, Lord, Thorp and Wilson, 2015) [**'IF THOU...'**] Of unknown provenance. [**FIVE-AND-SIXTY**] In his glossary, William Dickinson makes especial mention of the large number of synonyms for a 'strike' or 'blow' in the Cumbrian dialect. (*A Glossary of Words and Phrases pertaining to the Dialect of Cumberland*, William Dickinson, 1878.)

Emmer (Triticum dicoccum Schübl.)
Spelt (Triticum spelta L.)
Rug (Secale cereale L.)
Nøg. Byg (Hordeum tetrastichum Kcke., f. nudum)
Dækket Byg (Hordeum tetrastichum Kcke.)
Dyrket Havre (Avena sativa L.)
Flyvehavre (Avena fatua L.)
Grøn Skærmaks (Setaria viridis (L.) Beauv.)
Hanespore (Echinochloa crus-galli (L.) Beauv.)
Rottehale (Phleum sp.)
Fløjlsgræs (Holcus lanatus L.)
Mosebunke (Deschampsia caespitosa (L.) Beauv.)
Tagrør (Phragmites communis Trin.)
Tandlbælg (Sieglingia decumbens (L.) Bernh.)
Lund-Rapgræs (Poa nemoralis L.)
Rapgræs (Poa sp.)
Blød Hejre (Bromus mollis L.)
Almindelig Rajgræs (Lolium perenne L.)
Hør-Rajgræs (Lolium remotum Schrank)
Hundekvik (Agropyron caninum (L.) R. et S.)
Hare-Star (Carex leporina L.)
Markfrytle (Luzula campestris (L.) DC.)
Kruset Skræppe (Rumex crispus L.)
Rødknæ (Rumex acetosella L.)
Bleg Pileurt (Polygonum lapathifolium agg.)
Ferskenbladet Pileurt (Polygonum persicaria L.)
Vejpileurt (Polygonum aviculare L.)
Snerle-Pileurt (Polygonum convolvulus L.)

Hvidmelet Gåsefod (Chenopodium album L.)
Gåsefod (Chenopodium sp.)
Alm. Hønsetarm (Cerastium caespitosum Gilib.)
Græsbladet Fladstjerne (Stellaria graminea L.)
Alm. Fuglegræs (Stellaria media L.)
Enårig Knavel (Scleranthus annuus L.)
Alm. Spergel (Spergula arvensis L.)
Bidende Ranunkel (Ranunculus acris L.)
Lav Ranunkel (Ranunculus repens L.)
Læge Jordrøg (Fumaria officinalis L.)
Sæd-Dodder (Camelina lincola Sch. et Sp.)[1]
Ager-Pengeurt (Thlaspi arvense L.)
Hyrdetaske (Capsella Bursa-pastoris (L.) Moench)
Gyldenlak-Hjørnek. (Erysimum cheiranthoides L.)
Liden Løvefod (Aphanes arvensis L.)
Sølv-Potentil (Potentilla argentea L.)
Opret Potentil (Potentilla erecta (L.) Hampe)
Gul Kløver (Trifolium campestre Schreb.)
Fin Kløver (Trifolium dubium Sibth.)
Alm. Hør (Linum usitatissimum L.)
Ager-Stedmoderblomst (Viola arvensis Murr.)
Mark-Forglemmigej (Myosotis arvensis (L.) Hill)
Alm. Brunelle (Prunella vulgaris L.)
Alm. Hanekro (Galeopsis tetrahit agg.)
Sort Natskygge (Solanum nigrum L.)
Glat Ærenpris (Veronica serpyllifolia L.)
Skjaller (Rhinanthus cf. minor L.)
Glat Vejbred (Plantago major L.)

Lancetbladet Vejbred (Plantago lanceolata L.)
Nøgleblomstret Klokke (Campanula glomerata L.)
Finbladet Røllike (Achillea millefolium L.)
Lugtløs Kamille (Matricaria inodora L.)
Haremad (Lapsana communis L.)
Høst-Borst (Leontodon autumnalis L.)
Ru Svinemælk (Sonchus asper (L.) Hill)
Tag-Høgeskæg (Crepis tectorum L.)
Grøn Høgeskæg (Crepis capillaris (L.) Wallr.)

*

bang—to beat
bat—a blow, a stroke
batter—to strike repeatedly
bash away!—strike vigorously
beàsst—to beat
beat—to thrash with fist or stick
bensal—to beat
blāa—a blow
bray—to bruise or beat
bump—a blow
clink—a sharp blow
clonk—a sounding blow
cloot—a blow not repeated
cob—to kick
cuff—to strike without malice
dander—a blow on the head

dang—to push or strike
ding—to knock
down—to knock down
drub—to thrash
dump—to butt with the head
dust—to beat till dust rises
flail—to hit with a down stroke
floor—to knock down
fluet—a smart blow
hide—to beat the skin or hide
hit—to strike
kelk—to hit roughly with the hand, elbow, knee or foot
knock—a hard blow
lam—to beat
ledder—to beat
lig at—to strike at
mash—to disfigure by blows
nap—a slight blow to the head
nope—to strike on the head
pay—to beat
peg—a thump with the fist
pelk—to beat
pum, pummel—to pound or beat with the fists
quilt—to beat keenly
rap—a hard stroke
scop—to hit with a stone, or by a sling
skelp—to whip or beat
slap—to beat with the open hand

slouch—a blow clumsily struck
smack—a stroke on the face with the open hand
smash—to break a man down
spankin'—a clever beating
tap—a sharp stroke on the head
tan—to belabour the body
thud—a heavy blow with a dull sound
thump—a hard stroke with the fist
towel—to beat with a stick
trounce—to punish by beating
twilt—to beat keenly
wallop—to beat roughly
weft—to beat
whack—a strong and sounding blow
whale—to apply a cudgel
whap, whop—a smart blow
whelk—a thump with the fist
wipe—a back-handed stroke
yark—the fiercest of blows

SOURCES: *Grauballemandens Sidste Måltid*, Hans Helbæk, 1958; *A Glossary of Words and Phrases pertaining to the Dialect of Cumberland*, William Dickinson, 1878.

1 Sæd-Dodder (*Camelina sativa*).

THE CONTINENTAL WOULD

The paleomagnetic pendant of Europe hominins—a known engraving of older Lower Europe. Subsequent complex of record motif. The evolution fragments are whole genome reassembled. Mutliple caution at modern paleolatitude. Possible authors of Rodinia. Assessment of lineages for pigments. A rare peninsula used in the Mesolithic proposes primitive artefacts and renewed populations.

'BARBED LIVING EARTH MADE'

Enlarged and engraved using Neoproterozoic analytical styles. Hominin mtDNA—the mitochondrial string. 1.0 million years remain together with timing uncertainties. Worn by lineages the living pieced Neolithic affinities. The fossil supercontinent reassembled; a living Pannotia. Strung future. Multiple records uncovered. Little proposed.

BROKE SIMILAR UNTIL POORLY PIECED FIRST

Fossil archaic pendants. Early remains and spread of Rodinia. The peninsula warranting her fragments. Rapid years and rare. Microwear along early Britain in refugia. Pangaea states. Relevant sediments. The lower scientific key. Rapid global-scale humans. Here known yet the earliest star artwork. Tectonic exhibit. First described little femora. Collisional.

PIT ASSEMBLAGE CARNIVORES

Oxytocin burials show but broader animal peoples discovered. Rite patterns indicate support in bedrock. Pit mystery carnivore provides a culture of damage. Souls found in behaviour. A mutual primitive.

WILL 'SOULS' RESULT IN INCREASED EXISTENCE?

The ancient attempt. Hominins communicating emotionally. The tending of wolves. Urinary gazing. Possible histories. Death in northern years.

THE 'COMING ON' OF SOULS

Small ago. The least wounds in gazing. Repeated of signs. Northern occlusals. Purposeful burials. 'Souls' breakage. Modes of animals. Wolves into eye dogs. Human-like. Manipulatory.

WHAT SHAFT OCCUR ANIMALS?

The accident of blunt anatomy. Extinct rites. Small murder. Hapless. Animal bones. Human femur. Canid feet. Similar wrists. The fallen healing.

CANID YEARS:

Basal landscapes of human-animal contact.
Interspecies cemeteries.
Mortuary concepts.
Human-dog burials.
Wolf lineages.
Osteobiographies.
Combined histories.
Mitochondrial.

THE HYPOTHESES:

The 'within' muscle—the interior ritualised, scanning souls, skull cultures, exact gazing. The 'within' prior as animal existence. Souls' use of headdresses, antler techniques, pit manners, hand held. Labouring artefact techniques into breakages. Deer understanding. Diverging marks captured. Antler side blade, paleo-jaw-lake, bone modification: the male marks covered burials in the lower world.

Flint animal significance. The crania of deer, wolves. Barbed soul fragments. Clay dogs. Blunted rites. The 'core' complete in the Mesolithic—the study of small creation. Scholars of oral cut deer. Wolf-fight. Headdresses into peeled wrists. Spear-like. Wearing.

1157–63 haft three of skin to headdresses, found in appearance to be establishing ergotism.
1246 Belatucairus is waterlogged, part silver, in refugia. Some England of 1,000 man. The remains of a passage over water.
Wild by form with animal valleys. Tagrør dated to 43–410.
1252 Høgeskæg remains. The netherward first adult.

First sativa of wolves circle resemblance. Preservation holes. Multiple cords certain. Meal occupation between skull ridges.
1327 Fournes-fell: a local body. Falls of ryegrass. Animals into blood. The Duddon will awaken.
Pit writers, snow moss, spread headdress, nine body of preserved fossil. 'Millefolium and river.'
The other pine cave, now in neck of ruins, a Palaeolithic morass. The reburied tool. In bones unusual.

Lower human cultures. Hunting organizing a pattern. Fiercest in metamorphism.
Hem the art was rye, was birch. Repaired star muscle. Boar statue. Red gazing.
British etymology. Ornaments of þu. Calcined. Biometric trichiura.
The Scaleby vitrified shaft. The gedydon deposit of nine martens.

England clearly prefaces: surface bogs, slopes, hairs. Cave-bear. Yew. Dragons.
Alluvial surroundings. Water instruments. Fourneys scar analysis. Australopith-like.
The archaic 13. The derivation road. Body lineages.
Acts of stones. Bow woven. The cut detail. Outbursts of pottery.

THE PROXIMAL-BRITISH

The island alive of torn ground, throwing mountains, numerous, fast. A phalanx of culture; the northernmost language of place—marks, fronts, grasping posts, blood cubits. Albion cut into Britain, hurled, snatching, enraged, the shape of new ribs. Words made of small tools hung around bear islands, wolf jewellery, hyena caves. Evidence of the proximal-British—little greater art, oak notches, edge-smoothed talons, abrasions—polishing the gods.

A LITANY OF CULTS

cult of the alder
cult of the antlers
cult of the ash-throat
cult of the birch
cult of the birds
cult of the blood
cult of the blue people
cult of the boar
cult of the burning
cult of the carnal bogs
cult of the carrion
cult of the charred remains
cult of the clay dogs
cult of the clover
cult of the cradleland
cult of the cut marks
cult of the deer
cult of the Duddon
cult of the echoes
cult of the elder
cult of the elm decline
cult of the ergotism
cult of the fallow
cult of the figurines
cult of the five-and-sixty
cult of the great mother
cult of the grit-tooth
cult of the hatchlings

cult of the holy shales
cult of the horns
cult of the islands
cult of the juniper
cult of the karstic spear
cult of the killed valleys
cult of the lichen
cult of the lineages
cult of the lithic wounds
cult of the lower world
cult of the lowlands
cult of the mountains
cult of the nine martens
cult of the oak
cult of the pale north
cult of the peat bodies
cult of the plaited hair
cult of the pollen
cult of the provinces
cult of the red gazing
cult of the river
cult of the rye
cult of the salt
cult of the sea
cult of the seed
cult of the small wounds
cult of the snow
cult of the talons

cult of the tributary bones
cult of the vitrified shaft
cult of the willow
cult of the wolf
cult of the wormwood
cult of the yarrow
cult of the yew
cult of the young cases
cult of the Younger Dryas

FOLLOW THE HARE-STAR

the earthen second / thrash water / axe dialects / strong butchery / a new species of forest / the removed tributary / basal ruin / bog animals / fog phonation / a generous abundance / sediment chorus / peat bodies / nine the birds / stratigraphic boundaries / hazel the perfect headdress / border rituals / trace the range of women / found salt water / deep fallow limestones / horn clothing / horns fallen, findings / boar clover / sewn clay / wrist the traces / wolf crania *fallow* birds

perfect boundaries

boar sediment

tributary dialects

ruin found

[thrice the animals sang]

archaeopteryges

bird of the north

born

of snow carrion

bring

the white desert

the slow bright river

rivulet	*phonation*	*treatment*	*iconography*
stonework	*carbonized*	*fuvig*	*accident*
divided	*lorblanchet*	*sheepskins*	*component*
skeletal	*impoverishing*	*pharyngeal*	*affinities*
lac	*hylr*	*disappearance*	*subside*
duddon	*holocene*	*bromus*	*incentive*
lateglacial	*harewort*	*breaks*	*flint*
c.m.	*elm*	*method*	*vicinity*
armour	*woodlands*	*prodigious*	*bugge*
roum	*glacially*	*reoccupation*	*inwards*
april	*north-western*	*wastwater*	*possession*
twenty-five	*closed*	*focused*	*morphology*
disorder	*cervical*	*microscopic*	*enantiornithes*
human-like	*complementary*	*arvense*	*for*
blanks	*croatia*	*tempting*	*discoveries*
leàss	*moot*	*exceptionally*	*ledder*
southern	*caledonian*	*bear*	*person*
require	*murnende*	*substituted*	*barbs*
nope	*laterally*	*suggesting*	*referred*

something
breaks
glacially
a flint
incentive
a
morphology
of
possession

flattened	*earne*	*revealed*	*name*
make	*race*	*archaeologists*	*isochrone*
towel	*apart*	*considerable*	*sancto*
cities	*rout*	*food*	*stretch*
position	*widespread*	*dig*	*trim*
kent	*encampment*	*interment*	*himself*
cheeks	*purpose*	*clastic*	*almost*
finders	*embryo*	*generally*	*vertebrae*
moisture	*network*	*forness*	*ingleborough*
theropod	*peak*	*plumulaceous*	*antrim*
persicaria	*brocavum*	*lengths*	*gloria*
precocial	*enumeration*	*neatly*	*proto-solutrean*
intestines	*fixing*	*carnivores*	*leechdom*
extremes	*global-scale*	*coffin*	*beautiful*
considerably	*savage*	*ages*	*encourage*
caudal	*eveny*	*encounters*	*belatocairo*
body	*continuously*	*deadly*	*traces*
describe	*october*	*mobility*	*deluge*
scratch	*isoline*	*styrr*	*aurochs*

			bedrock
soil		sulphur	
	defleshed	matrix	
	marls		
those	*profile*	*glimpses*	*chopped*
heat	*preserve*	*light*	*adult*
greatly	*sat*	*perenne*	*meadow*
intus	*etc.*	*required*	*cemeteries*
peoples	*histories*	*once*	*non-calcareous*
portion	*diagrammatic*	*scale*	*numbers*
posteriorly	*kre'k*	*douglas*	*beliefs*
bloom	*ravelrig*	*belt*	*luguvalium*
fuder	*number*	*matrix*	*macrophotography*
persisted	*performance*	*datasets*	*femur*
hyrdetaske	*cloot*	*lowland*	*remote*
coincides	*decomposition*	*communis*	*pleasure*
arguably	*d.n.a.*	*provide*	*belong*
wearing	*moults*	*greek*	*forming*
modification	*standard*	*colonisation*	*cervus*
dried	*germany*	*gloves*	*battle*
butchery	*second-century*	*speleothem*	*case*
analytical	*massacree*	*friday*	*characteristics*
camden	*birks*	*sinews*	*demonstrating*
bishopwort	*by*	*two*	*probability*
national	*chipped*	*mentions*	*cowlow*
natskygge	*chief*	*killed*	*degree*
inside	*north-west*	*aquatic*	*pieced*
pack	*bathing*	*and*	*provided*
repetitive	*fly*	*coats*	*or*
epoch	*lithic*	*groove*	*protohistorical*

brief

hammers

northern

lines

mallow	*confirmed*	*font*	*rug*
alkaloids	*movement*	*demise*	*paleo-lake*
silver	*geology*	*consume*	*vipers*
coated	*horizons*	*consist*	*plains*

the fiercest of blows

pits	*virtue*	*district*	*manipulations*
see	*lœge*	*dug*	*superprecocial*
children	*malice*	*goat*	*denu*
pictographic	*so-called*	*tiny*	*multi-level*

blunt

bewitchment			*pay*
apprehending			*microtus*
boreal			*omnium*
database			*above*
whale	*circumference*	*topography*	*barbules*
breathing	*fu*	*temperatures*	*general*
bone-ash	*australopith-like*	*kings*	*hair*
ru	*angle*	*fenland*	*resuscitated*
colonise	*islands*	*latin*	*mary*
elliptical	*lovage*	*du*	*results*
lig	*mid-cretaceous*	*rounded*	*centre*
limit	*boundary*	*deaths*	*because*
collisional	*through*	*ruins*	*thongs*
goëmagots	*jordrøg*	*exterior*	*think*
commerce	*layers*	*grasses*	*nidderdale*
factor	*netherby*	*extended*	*barb*
vestige	*real*	*peat*	*corruption*
deposited	*juniper*	*regum*	*renderings*
branches	*scenario*	*rows*	*imaging*
horizontal	*reindeer*	*irreconcilable*	*mind*
literature	*grauballe*	*grazing*	*blakeney*
gazing	*asymmetrical*	*taken*	*klokke*

topography

	gael	*million*	
	bottom	*blelham*	
	including	*ossified*	
	another	*joints*	
everywhere	*essentially*	*peaks*	*coverts*
buxton	*link*	*anterad*	*mousterian*
settlements	*refugia*	*least*	*functioned*
leven	*seventeenth*	*elder*	*hands*
mon	*festival*	*oblivion*	*gledes*
leuenam	*caesar*	*attire*	*products*
apex	*balatucairo*	*clothing*	*factors*
account	*average*	*base*	*alike*
dækket	*castalidum*	*garlic*	*diversity*
oval	*subsequently*	*europe*	*lack*
operating	*bat*	*plaited*	*sand*
dominant	*mint*	*rose*	*pax*
horn	*concentrations*	*staff*	*marls*
duthen	*braitha*	*he*	*various*
furnesio	*concerned*	*charred*	*visited*
kaimes	*english*	*beating*	*manipulatory*
triggered	*litany*	*reaches*	*officinalis*
ornament	*america*	*consuming*	*next*

snow-charred

carr	*brassicaceae*	*erupt*	*scandinavia*
similar	*style*	*bare*	*fouldrey*
parish	*triticum*	*spear-like*	*goëmagot*
muscle	*minor*	*drains*	*open*
british	*comparison*	*exhibit*	*heather*
darker	*ameliorated*	*lincola*	*locate*
characterised	*drained*	*nocturnal*	*specialists*
occlusive	*curated*	*dub*	*interspersed*
guide	*night*	*eadwacer*	*ossification*
scope	*burial*	*clues*	*dentibus*
furthermore	*dominated*	*forwarding*	*consisted*
include	*coverage*	*beads*	*trailing*
cambrian	*severed*	*countenance*	*dynasties*
ornithuromorphs	*tree*	*drink*	*dental*
form	*extremity*	*dragged*	*deposit*
surmised	*collision*	*usitatissimum*	*letter*
dump	*amend*	*created*	*manual*
star	*choice*	*covert*	*butchered*
regarding	*belatucatro*	*rolley*	*previous*
advance	*ill*	*ergotoxicosis*	*pagan*
allow	*joint*	*cassuck*	*cooling*
claw	*consider*	*sore*	*terræ*
post-date	*inhabitants*	*pendant*	*radiometric*
muscles	*pennulum*	*thickness*	*infilling*
from	*arctic-alpine*	*exposure*	*confines*
lepus	*nightshade*	*approaching*	*sinew*
steers	*mid-cumbria*	*desire*	*completely*
common	*grams*	*shrouded*	*sublingua*
nails	*arable*	*millennia*	*recasting*
articulates	*ergotism*	*belonging*	*neatness*
talons	*gåsefod*	*indistinctly*	*ninety-one*

ridges

fallen
region
milky
slowed
climate
rectrices
featuring
attached
items
convolvulus
belatucadro
iceman
grip
negotiate
assembled
decline
sing
moved
basis
situated
flap
estimates
published
gorge
acting
nostri
otter
over
awaken
archaic
why
rapgræs
material
materials
convincing
acute
around
ornamented
tollund
nemoralis
cognate
exploratorum
sip
cob
mineral
endocranial
wreaths
proximal
worn
settlement
vadose
stratigraphy
art
grease
places
unique
antlers
inurned
close
became
fragments
reduced
treasure
reconstruct
lað
græsbladet
reached
forests
dips
language
something
treeline
past
opposed
grassington
contracted
ground
cradle
pillars
apices
creation
mid-holocene
writing
no-one
prolonged
microstructure
stanton
dubh
approach
ninth
pterylosis
remnants
wyld
analyses
peak
enantiornithines
dicoccum
cane
recurved
genetic
circumstances
corylus
then
caused
buttercup
glyceria
hyena
somewhat
peats
proposed
arrows
cumberland
certain
widely
kachin
missing
labouring
lor
unction
restore
relevant
tight
flake-removal
mouth

pendants of bracing quick sediment

neonatal	*includes*	*margins*	*block*
pulled	*tanai*	*apparently*	*poorly*
piece	*coast*	*highlands*	*bring*
heavy	*contexts*	*discussions*	*albion*
secondaries	*bowl*	*fossil*	*phosphoric*
javelin	*sheepskin*	*outstanding*	*membrorum*
reduce	*consonant*	*ediacaran*	*osterby*
occurs	*effective*	*icons*	*unearthed*
among	*fish*	*rendered*	*do*
colour	*balance*	*scarcity*	*underdeveloped*
madrid	*ranges*	*bird*	*laurentide*
continuity	*cessation*	*gesomnad*	*amongst*
feathers	*scientific*	*roe*	*collected*
attempting	*maple*	*ötzal*	*complex*
delve	*chiefly*	*life*	*protrude*
opening	*baited*	*growing*	*gul*
trojan	*bank*	*blade-like*	*tan*
lies	*apparent*	*trunk*	*roused*
holes	*ontogenetic*	*whether*	*solely*

cult of the cut marks

evenki
seems
birth
equal
marrow
brunelle
thursday
commonest
afterwards
eurasia
lanceolata
similarly
clumsily
foxes
dudda
goemagot
livid
online
many

existence
analysed
ladder
alm
maker
identified
comparing
attack
lacked
otrepole
ywedalebec
knoll
argentea
abounds
perished
þær
regeneration
wheel
firm

leap
threads
flyvehavre
names
major
unlike
hearth
surrounding
reveal
yew
manus
me
current
barbed
blue
fōðor
mostly
reports
nitrogen

benedicite
knees
løvefod
prevailing
lupin
elf
ash
cape
put
damage
lain
eagle
ruchmoor
substantiate
sedge
finder
happen
great
sourced

fragments aiming distal thrash

doncaster	*pour*	*commander*	*also*
baliticauro	*keeping*	*interpretations*	*yewdale*
coincided	*conjecture*	*keep*	*question*
lebby	*mark*	*assessing*	*pummel*
not	*geador*	*hydrology*	*scalar-shaped*
publication	*retained*	*dating*	*mourners*
maryport	*mapping*	*colouration*	*topographically*
values	*seams*	*charms*	*cleaved*
piskeorm	*abrupt*	*encouraged*	*mixture*
mud	*rooting*	*necklace*	*constrictor*
avena	*anomala*	*cross-sectional*	*collection*
tandlbælg	*caninum*	*carefully*	*leather*
act	*onto*	*bygbr*	*pre-roman*
auribus	*quick*	*þæt*	*allows*
caespitosa	*smaller*	*resembling*	*one*
model	*belatucadros*	*collect*	*commences*
belabour	*freres*	*furnais*	*demineralised*
challenges	*highly*	*gave*	*mature*
green	*antlered*	*notion*	*avialan*

cult of the lithic wounds

period	*neither*	*no*	*person-divine*
headdress	*successive*	*commend*	*karren*
classification	*had*	*acts*	*clowe*
precambrian	*minimising*	*preservation*	*fornesio*
comparable	*mixed*	*promoted*	*day*
prelithic	*cairns*	*mask*	*pyrotechnology*
markedly	*fossils*	*large-scale*	*collaging*
northeastern	*morass*	*haplogroups*	*throughout*
violent	*expressive*	*cymric*	*x-ray*
finer	*substances*	*celt*	*planting*
days	*orogeny*	*villages*	*fatua*
humanity's	*carried*	*groups*	*berre*
representative	*agriculture*	*hurled*	*originate*
fingers	*perfection*	*occupants*	*languages*
conservet	*sores*	*enclosure*	*kirkby*
sections	*anthropogenic*	*institute*	*precipitation*
thrice	*lost*	*nights*	*infers*
converted	*correct*	*appear*	*de-skinning*
overridden	*fodernesio*	*manner*	*insurmountable*

a scar mosaic

lykkja	*establishment*	*software*	*periods*
half	*composed*	*assessment*	*season*
arierge	*periglacial*	*restricted*	*wales*
cared	*limits*	*enquiries*	*isotope*
drachenloch	*campanula*	*near*	*modelling*
motif	*tag-høgeskæg*	*records*	*branch*
bone	*pollen*	*must*	*coincident*
sword	*rachises*	*refugial*	*split*
camboglanna	*ear*	*mash*	*due*
positive	*dove*	*alluvial*	*pleasant*
kirkbride	*extend*	*bounded*	*anything*
wæs	*mcclure*	*burgh-by-sands*	*aphanes*
pigments	*mesh*	*obscured*	*township*
vertebrates	*incisions*	*mystery*	*on*
documented	*salt*	*ago*	*succeeding*
attach	*wælreowe*	*breakup*	*punish*
carboniferous	*inches*	*combined*	*interacting*
produced	*finsthwaite*	*go*	*represent*
borne	*cave-bear*	*responsible*	*dichotomy*

all
mythologies
and
archives
extinct

signifying	*scrapers*	*expelle*	*being*
certainly	*pathway*	*fairly*	*blank*
cymeð	*earliest*	*digastric*	*communicating*
rudolfensis	*decreasing*	*laser*	*myitkyina*
marquet	*stored*	*adjective*	*ask*
archaeopteryx	*scar*	*trimmed*	*mosaic*
better	*haunted*	*moving*	*perspective*
rest	*context*	*blocked*	*trap*
alula	*instead*	*generously*	*it*
pavements	*ærenpris*	*gruel*	*no[illegible]ter*
cartilage	*further*	*minum*	*knee*
royal	*college*	*itself*	*defining*
classed	*eye*	*grykes*	*ranunkel*
prevented	*row*	*wounds*	*boar*
reconstructions	*manufacturing*	*remnant*	*deflected*
leg	*nes*	*neandertal*	*retention*
details	*trochlear*	*area*	*so[illegible]s*
warranting	*forty*	*extinction*	*necessary*
according	*face*	*terminates*	*sa[illegible]e*

mitochondrial amber

mineral souls

artemisia	*defended*	*dominate*	*otterpool*
away	*owners*	*lash*	*mire*
sølv-potentil	*miscellaneous*	*believe*	*posture*
radius	*belatucauro*	*playne*	*scotland*
grange	*echinochloa*	*relationship*	*targe*

collision water
stadial ruin
lifeways broken

made

ordovician	*analogous*	*quite*	*mouldered*
seem	*physiological*	*tumulus*	*variety*
articulated	*knavel*	*depictions*	*diarthrodial*
compound	*piled*	*foudray*	*studied*
alien	*living*	*where*	*figurines*

caves keeping the great clover

platform	*croglinhurst*	*earnestly*	*paler*
metallurgy	*elfthone*	*airway*	*active*
mesozoic	*kamille*	*gaze*	*hath*
distally	*insights*	*hyoeides*	*pre-boreal*
permanent	*wands*	*push*	*plateaux*
signum	*deserve*	*attributable*	*back*
soul	*digits*	*subcontinent*	*says*
mean	*mayst*	*extensively*	*bones*
represents	*hazel*	*basal*	*sapeornis*
monthly	*truly*	*glass*	*jewellery*
blocks	*ilk*	*occurrences*	*balanced*
martes	*expedient*	*leading*	*resources*
emphasis	*windswept*	*humankind*	*cold-tolerant*
replaced	*strip*	*although*	*gaps*
arrow	*surrounded*	*district*	*isle*
approximately	*controlling*	*placed*	*phenomena*
cerastium	*restricts*	*rib*	*arctic*
indices	*european*	*fine*	*landed*
tapering	*passes*	*withers*	*ankylosed*
giant	*warfare*	*remarkable*	*brathey*
grooves	*relied*	*limestones*	*lifeways*
prehistory	*patterning*	*taper*	*documentation*
role	*depth*	*revisits*	*outbreaks*
examination	*winstirthwaytes*	*leporina*	*fingernail*
halter	*identifies*	*modern-looking*	*fotherey*
ustilago	*especially*	*bed*	*bechsteini*
twelve	*patination*	*purchased*	*eruption*

refugial glimpses

dominantium	*earthen*	*ancestors*	*description*
precludes	*france*	*capillis*	*paper*
skin	*possible*	*paintings*	*compliments*
russian	*anthropology*	*penrith*	*studying*
eight	*former*	*hatchet*	*ditch*
directions	*stick*	*intensity*	*health*
knife	*wolf*	*penyghent*	*dudn*
lancetbladet	*bracing*	*crouching*	*sudden*
expected	*belief*	*trees*	*woods*
point	*fumaria*	*call*	*rivers*
remaining	*anaerobic*	*rain*	*arch*
distantly	*pure*	*moisten*	*hare*
classified	*fully*	*paternoster*	*prospect*
brief	*detestable*	*russia*	*socio-religious*
noted	*scavenging*	*stem*	*frontal*
lye	*sometimes*	*displacement*	*happened*
encounter	*habitats*	*prepatagium*	*lodged*
luzula	*archetypes*	*eriophorum*	*crust*
repeatedly	*subtle*	*anatolian*	*rules*
relict	*markings*	*the*	*craft*
java	*caespitosum*	*play*	*supplied*
hyoid	*adequate*	*dreadful*	*changing*
clonk	*mortuary*	*support*	*thin*
prevailed	*waves*	*vivipara*	*genomic*
blood	*presents*	*brutus*	*staffordshire*
based	*bulrushes*	*shade-intolerant*	*information*
gedydon	*its*	*carnal*	*unable*

living ligament
emerging

	semblance	*belatucairus*	
vary	*confuciusornis*	*schematic*	*extraction*
cooked	*preventing*	*awareness*	*imperatives*
older	*wreathed*	*panted*	*twelvemonth*
viridis	*skærmaks*	*whack*	*urn*
inherent	*below*	*abandonment*	*investigate*
classic	*wet*	*ashthroat*	*rachis*
traditionally	*sickles*	*dramatic*	*rapine*
main	*scraping*	*supercontinent*	*space*
questions	*freezing*	*white*	*catchments*
linguists	*rex*	*hill*	*there*
spain	*b.p.*	*rygh*	*meltwater*
thud	*transformation*	*ran*	*sedimentary*
particle	*heigh*	*suppose*	*pennines*
again	*limbs*	*palaeo*	*feather*
compassion	*oil*	*-environmental*	*minimum*
geological	*experience*	*vessel*	*commenced*
obstructing	*dill*	*æternam*	*development*
sindon	*wyn*	*till*	*elbows*
beneath	*upfolded*	*pigment*	*fudeholmen*
suggestions	*israel*	*size*	*hør-rajgræs*
designated	*scripts*	*dalmahoy*	*knock*
mountainous	*penncreic*	*anatomy*	*corresponds*
os	*cornua*	*lines*	*magico-religious*

cult of the mother

cult of the hatchlings

cult of the young cases

lie			*horns*
pursuing	*eat*	*sides*	*whatever*
at	*tentatively*	*gife*	*represented*
debris	*inclusion*	*turf*	*proved*
clink	*arvensis*	*torn*	*hand*
glaciation	*himalayan*	*trouble*	*halves*
anterior	*polygonum*	*five*	*vigorously*
swanscombe	*solanum*	*demonstrate*	*bathe*
snow-filled	*northern*	*detached*	*location*
closer	*digitally*	*elaphus*	*rectugu*
deceased	*home*	*cultural*	*between*
seed	*know*	*accurate*	*cerebro*
mines	*plumage*	*galway*	*exploiting*
elevation	*infirmis*	*lived*	*intermittent*
closely	*disciplines*	*palaeolithic*	*tough*
thrashing	*species-rich*	*probably*	*lofty*
juvenile	*shale*	*involves*	*lacking*
thy	*lickin*	*farmed*	*soul-flights*
mollis	*molecular*	*waste*	*suggest*

the solemn seed
crouching in
carcasses

sings

strata	*rites*	*desirous*	*hunt*
credo	*remove*	*symbolic*	*damendorf*
loosely	*continues*	*concept*	*acetosella*
silence	*goosefoot*	*hundred*	*resin*
canis	*shakeholes*	*leaves*	*highlights*
derivative	*injury*	*unburnt*	*best*
crucis	*underground*	*talon*	*plants*
coloured	*religious*	*copper*	*furness*
swylce	*altar*	*embedded*	*moreover*
whip	*produce*	*fact*	*nøg*
elk	*ergot*	*preceded*	*dudene*
incorporation	*core*	*sufficiently*	*demonstrates*
looketh	*winter*	*improve*	*reddish*
micro-vertebrate	*attention*	*patch*	*mouse*
wider	*wenum*	*bodies*	*axe*
group	*centuries*	*variants*	*deeply*
exploration	*cannot*	*humerus*	*porcelain*
svinemælk	*divide*	*yet*	*costume*
breath	*suprahyoid*	*displayed*	*intended*

archaeopteryges

bird of the north

born

of wet lineages

come

lay the inundation

costume

us in water

discoverer	*receiving*	*positionem*	*klover*
impact	*pharynx*	*hoc*	*whole*
spergula	*bi-directional*	*amber*	*thyself*
high-resolution	*marrubium*	*articular*	*hippophäe*
hammers	*småster*	*individual*	*tissue*
frameworks	*enhance*	*invasion*	*cumbria*
propose	*devil*	*emanate*	*indicator*
earnest	*chenopodium*	*unclear*	*discrepancies*
decaying	*holding*	*conclusive*	*glyptic*
westmorland	*derrykeighhan*	*efforts*	*sound*
decumbens	*alternating*	*changed*	*yarrow*
blāa	*glutinous*	*empties*	*follow*
deschampsia	*murder*	*tanning*	*cowhide*
gods	*secale*	*though*	*moorland*
belatucbro	*medial*	*resistant*	*sire*
poor	*states*	*rozzel*	*spectacular*
occur	*prepare*	*bash*	*animal*
hundreds	*carvoran*	*afield*	*strength*
exploit	*wort*	*ape-like*	*same*

THE RULES SET LOW (I)

meseums in apex earth

bones breathing quick clay

pendants to the swallowing interstadial second

fragments and earthen strong

notches to bracing tongue

genomes have keeping wild salt

and membrane bodies

CRADLELAND

Broken pollen. The records in the peat. Furness grown fallow. The first fog of animals encountered. The Duddon shrouded all that is west of the boar. A find in the lungs. Broad blows of karstic, wrapped in the wild source. Bones wormed the crania, bearing provinces, split bogs, amber docks. Location taxa: the first word, *birch*, is attested. Hazel remains a life hormone, found in perfect traces in most branches of Indo-European. Bark dialects. Leaf costumes. The old rubrics. 'The meaning of words change such that we cannot be sure of the original meaning of words we reconstruct.'

['THE MEANINGS OF WORDS ...'] Colin Renfrew, quoted in *In Search of the Indo-Europeans, Language, Archaeology and Myth*, J.P. Mallory (1991).

THE FELLS HAVE MUCH MASK

North of the pale lowlands. Basal forests, resin sheets. North of oak, elm, ash. The sparse age of slowed pollen. North of body counterparts. Dark sites around wood moults. North of the wild mention of deities. The holy history declines.

'We are incomplete to describe the north': Indices of the boar. Fluted pendants of the cult islands. Small evidence of outer species. Are these the bone communities, the women and men whose finders are burning?

['WE ARE INCOMPLETE ...'] Of unknown provenance.

THE ALULAR RESEARCH

Along the thorax range. Ungual ridges, dorsal forests. The sudden ditch has birds. Marginal flights, isle coverts. Here is the feather of years. Plumage sites, wing bedrock. Cliffs report the osteology of flight: 'hurled down the savage monster into the sea'. A northernmost evidence. A bracelet of talons.

['HURLED DOWN ...'] *The British History of Geoffrey of Monmouth*, J.A. Giles, 1842. [A BRACELET OF TALONS] cf. The Tomb of the Eagles, South Ronaldsay, Orkney, a Neolithic monument in which white-tailed sea eagle bones were found, among other birds and numerous human remains.

WILLOW COMMONEST PLENTIFUL

Salix of the four ways
        proximal, distal, ventral, dorsal.
Salix of the grey clearance
        birch episodes, alder hatchlings.
Salix of the dark central
        the grow of cotton and water.
Salix of the floodplains
        fen birds predict the elm decline.
Salix of the pale broad
        feathers of bog disturbance.

[THE ELM DECLINE] Occurred in the mid-Holocene, roughly 6,000 BP.

OF THE MAN IN THE MOSS

'Black is the palest colour, boiled in milk, becoming lighter. Dubh is made from yew compounds, sung over with nine masses. Duß is the black and burn of it, the countenance of the first seest. With an admixture of these three circle his neck, with it mark his head and chest, threefold.' They buried him not dead but living. A seed of a corpse, a promise. 'I have wreathed round the wounds the best of healing.' The man in the moss will awake, germinating, muttering.

[**PALEST COLOUR**] OE *blac* 'bright, shining, glittering, pale'. [**DUß**] Cumbric **duß, *dü,* 'black'. [**NINE MASSES**] cf. 'have nine masses sung over them', *Leech Book* III, LXII, in *Leechdoms, Wortcunning, and Starcraft of Early England*, Oswald Cockayne, 1865. [**'WITH AN ADMIXTURE...'**] Of unknown provenance. [**THREEFOLD**] cf. 'threefold death' (see notes to 'strong deaths', p. 119). [**'I HAVE WREATHED ...'**] *Leech Book* III, LXIII.

THE RULES SET LOW (II)

I

objects around found souls
like lingual antlers

II

feathers against proximal remains
grammars lesser sediment

III

caves ventral sewn
body; signum arch artefact

IIII

flattened thou the wings
by christs constrictor dorsal

IIIII
in water joints the
diagrams aiming quiver peat

I.I
for lichen and isolated
also are to bone

I.II
during chamber the resin
the contra of with

I.III
where the body findings
six the the the

THE FOUR WAYS

[proximal] I am plumage birch
[I am] sediment oak
[I am] fog clover

...

[I am clay]

...

[distal] I am upper waves
[I am] lingual sea
[I am] slow shore

...

[I am water]

...

[ventral] I am deer bone
[I am] downward feather
[I am] quick wolf

...

[I am death]

...

[dorsal] I am tongue chorus
[I am] ligament song
[I am] mitochondrial dialects

...

[I am language]

...

...

[I am] axe museums

...

...

[I am] absent elm

...

...

[I am] sphagnum levels

...

...

[I am] mineral bodies

...

...

[I am] thought forest

...

...

[I am] refugial body

...

...

[I am] blood rites

...

...

[I am] fallow

...

AN EVIDENCE

here the bones
the ashes of the dead
the articles of value

talons of salt
amber pendants
tongues of the downward sea

placed in the recesses
for use in the spirit world
the living slow borders

WHERE NOTHING ESCAPES

we stand together
glyphs of fingers
weigh ritual
in ruins

come lay
the inundation
we already
semblance death

STUDY OF SMALL CREATION

here known yet the earliest star artwork
cave-bear, extinct rites, drowned peninsulas
the accident of blunt anatomy

MUSEUMS IN APEX EARTH

ochre and salt
the crania of deer
barbed soul fragments
wolf lineages

THE RULES SET LOW (III)

(1)

before the drowned peninsulas

languages along mineral tissues
marks below border souls (mineral, arboreal, interstadial)
open boundaries, membrane rites
caves of the climatic sea

(ii)

the lower findings

tongue regions, downward sediment
birds of the karstic shore
small gods key open the dialects
grammars greater, deep

HYOIDOMANCY

to see the ligament world
betokens bodies
to see the welling night
betokens comets
to see the gone
betokens never so much blood
to see the pharynx sea
betokens earth
to see with stars
betokens bones, rivers
to see the diarthrodial wheel
betokens sapiens
to see round planets
betokens stars, veins
to see the incalculable
betokens heavenly speech
to see beneath fire
betokens constellations
to see sleep
betokens the very world

NOTE: Unlike others bones, the hyoid is only distantly articulated to its neighbours by muscles or ligaments. These prognostic statements, in the style of *The Book of Dreams* by Prophet Daniel, are likewise created from disarticulated materials. The title, 'Hyoidomancy', alludes to the ancient practice of divination using bones.

FOUND TRIBUTARY AREAS

ridges from setting slow
tributary lineages like
looking greater trees have
breathing open found
figurines below living greater
bodies levels with bracing
lower marls grammars with
being greater souls fragments
in late-apex sewn artefacts
around surrounding open
axe findings at surviving
wild tissues canines to
farming ventral earth
findings like looking lingual
fog dialects by surrounding
distal sewn figurines found
connecting lesser sewn
dialects tongue animals
talons between swallowing
alular plumage dialects of
the breathing whole soil
dialects towards patterning
quick animals hooklets
of aiming elm canines
are offering lesser rites
types along aiming found
remains grammars from
wearing open wolf objects

beneath being near grain
dialects below connecting
quick perfect hooklets
through late-earthen deep
figurines in looking slow
grain birds through aiming
arboreal rituals birds
along patterning medial
genomes like breathing
secondary grain foxes
around changing mineral
animals canines from being
found antlers caves have
not bracing secondary wing
lineages around patterning
refugial strong specimens
between wearing quiver
rituals populations have
flying central horn areas
to wearing upper clay
genomes past surrounding
lesser chorus ridges towards
living lesser crania hooklets
from extending lower
pendants around being
wild tributary dialects
before setting complete
butchery foxes around

bracing mitochondrial regions specimens below bracing far sea canines beneath swallowing medial clover types in patterning interstadial rituals dialects against mid-complete salt birds found extending primary butchery trees at late-climatic border hooklets over patterning primary specimens beneath flying tongue birds caves found breathing lesser animals birches under changing apex peat areas to the keeping quick horns levels from surviving earthen antlers canines across wearing ventral remains levels between farming inferior trace bones past swallowing greater hominins barbules at living complete horns lineages over mid-lower antlers canines and late-arboreal found levels around manufacturing

anterior sewn remains by sequencing wild marls woodlands are meaning found tributary areas to the offering karstic waves talons below early border phonation pendants against breathing mitochondrial butchery objects after flying far wrist foxes between living membrane trace marks to the patterning apex elm levels are not manufacturing upper hazel birds from surrounding border populations to the swallowing refugial deep lineages beneath fixing thought crania talons before being mineral boundaries species from sequencing complete nine artefacts between patterning upper water pendants around bracing primary butchery beneath surrounding proximal marls pendants to the throttling quick strong types across surviving absent salt notches at meaning near amber remains in sequencing quick water bones around late-arboreal crania populations before aiming central fields birches through early alular ruin trees towards breathing whole deer birches at late-alular shore bones and being articular removed woodlands to the bracing ligament tributary levels of mid-distal wing carcasses like surrounding refugial deep languages are not late-border grammars have not aiming climatic regions marks by offering near soil barbules have not offering quick boundaries caves and flying border phonation birds to the being ligament chorus

populations and fixing inferior sphagnum remains under keeping lingual fields caves of the manufacturing climatic salt grammars are not flying membrane fallen types to the connecting far dialects margins like bracing climatic hazel populations surviving medial blood species with extending articular boar specimens around living mineral wing canines below flying lesser peat areas found extending secondary traces museums to surrounding lesser clay talons breathing secondary water lineages towards meaning proximal ruin specimens to connecting anterior second birds have surviving vertebral earth ventral earth

·

lingual fog

·

dialects of the breathing whole soil

·

grain foxes

·

interstadial rituals

·

birches under changing apex peat

·

anterior sewn remains

·

living membrane trace marks to the patterning elm

·

mid-distal wing carcasses

·

refugial deep languages

·

late-border grammars

·

surviving

·

vertebral

THE FLYING OF TONGUES

the quick boundary of bird phonation
clay talons breathing towards meaning
to the offering karstic waves

OFFERING OF THE LESSER RITES

slow tributary lineages
wearing ventral remains
earthen antlers
quiver rituals

THE BODY FROM SCALEBY MOSS

25 May 1834

who is she
this residual this relique
her skin daubed a river's colour
her mind sieved and cased in the hide of a deer

remnants hand the bog tympanic
remnants hand the almost neck
the spine body
we now carry the corrupted word

and the soft putty of mosses
absent membranes
calcium throats
eye pouches

(peat formed from decaying plants
combined with humic and fulvic acids
and the residues of insects algae fungi)

insects
the pupal earth the soil her chrysalis
the cloak she gathered about herself
her pharate body

we have brought her out too early
too late to reinter her
to close the wound

the earth an instant for this leather bone woman
long in her dwelling her stained orbits
they called it birth they called it *the living after living*

anterior of the coronal country
mineral light
brain flora
daughter isotopes

and even the sun cannot explain
her unlit chambers of vision

LICHENOMETRY

Lichenometry [1] — [2] a [3] method [4] developed [5] by [6] geologists [7] for [8] dating [9] Holocene [10] moraines [11] and [12] other [13] landforms [14] — [15] has [16] many [17] potential [18] applications [19] in [20] archaeology. [21] Maximum-diameter [22] lichenometry [23] can [24] suggest [25] ages [26] for [27] features [28] that [29] were [30] initially [31] lichen-free, [32] such [33] as [34] the [35] moai [36] of [37] Easter [38] Island, [39] and [40] rock [41] surfaces [42] exposed [43] by [44] toolstone [45] quarrying. [46] Size-frequency [47] analysis [48] can [49] provide [50] dates [51] for [52] structures [53] built [54] of [55] lichen-covered [56] rocks, [57] such [58] as [59] game-drive [60] walls [61] and [62] blinds, [63] meat [64] caches, [65] and [66] tent [67] rings. [68] Both [69] methods [70] require [71] local [72] calibration [73] curves, [74] best [75] constructed [76] by [77] measuring [78] lichens [79] on [80] substrata [81] of [82] known [83] exposure [84] age. [85] Most [86] lichenometric [87] studies [88] have [89] involved [90] yellow [91] members [92] of [93] the [94] crustose [95] genus [96] Rhizocarpon, [97] which [98] grow [99] slowly [100] and [101] can [102] live [103] for [104] as [105] long [106] as [107] 10,000 [108] years. [109] Lichenometry [110] has [111] been [112] particularly [113] successful [114] on [115] siliceous [116] rock [117] types [118] in [119] arctic, [120] subarctic, [121] and [122] alpine-tundra [123] environments. [124] The [125] effects [126] of [127] wildfire [128] and [129] of [130] competition [131] from [132] foliose [133] lichens [134] make [135] the [136] technique [137] less [138] well [139] suited [140] for [141] forested [142] terrain. [143] Few [144] data [145] are [146] available [147] for [148] tropical [149] or [150] desert [151] environments [152] or [153] for [154] calcareous [155] substrata. [156] The [157] reliability [158] of [159] a [160] lichenometric [161] date [162] will [163] depend [164] on [165] the [166] quality [167] of [168] the [169] calibration [170] curve, [171] the [172] size [173] of [174] the [175] sample, [176] the [177] nature [178] and [179] postoccupational [180] history [181] of [182] the [183] substratum, [184] and [185] the [186] ability [187] of [188] the [189] archaeologist [190] to [191] recognize [192] potential [193] disturbance [194] factors. [195] An [196] ecological [197] perspective [198] is [199] essential. [200]

SOURCE: 'A Review of Lichenometric Dating and Its Application to Archaeology', James B. Benedict, *American Antiquity*, Vol 74 No 1, 2017.

— [2, 15] 10,000 [108] a [3, 160] ability [187] age. [85] ages [26] alpine-tundra [123] an [196] analysis [48] and [12, 40, 62, 66, 101, 122, 129, 179, 185] applications [19] archaeologist [190] archaeology. [21] arctic, [120] are [146] as [34, 59, 105, 107] available [147] been [112] best [75] blinds, [63] both [69] built [54] by [6, 44, 77] caches, [65] calcareous [155] calibration [73, 170] can [24, 49, 102] competition [131] constructed [76] crustose [95] curve, [171] curves, [74] data [145] date [162] dates [51] dating [9] depend [154] desert [151] developed [5] disturbance [194] easter [38] ecological [197] effects [126] environments [124, 152] essential. [200] exposed [43] exposure [84] factors. [195] features [28] few [144] foliose [133] for [8, 27, 52, 104, 141, 148, 154] forested [142] from [132] game-drive [60] genus [96] geologists [7] grow [99] has [16, 111] have [89] history [181] holocene [10] in [20, 119] initially [31] involved [90] is [199] island, [39] known [83] landforms [14] less [138] lichen-covered [56] lichen-free, [32] lichenometric [87, 161] lichenometry [1, 23, 110] lichens [79, 134] live [103] local [72] long [106] make [135] many [17] maximum-diameter [22] measuring [78] meat [64] members [92] method [4] methods [70] moai [36] moraines [11] most [86] nature [178] of [37, 55, 82, 93, 127, 130, 159, 168, 174, 182, 188] on [80, 115, 165] or [150, 53] other [13] particularly [113] perspective [198] postoccupational [180] potential [18, 193] provide [50] quality [167] quarrying. [46] recognize [192] reliability [158] require [71] rhizocarpon, [97] rings. [68] rock [47, 117] rocks, [57] sample, [176] siliceous [116] size [173] size-frequency [47] slowly [100] structures [33] studies [88] subarctic, [121] substrata [81, 156] substratum, [184] successful [114] such [33, 58] suggest [25] suited [140] surfaces [42] technique [137] tent [67] terrain. [143] that [29] the [35, 94, 125, 136, 157, 166, 169, 172, 175, 177, 183, 186, 189] to [191] toolstone [45] tropical [149] types [118] walls [61] well [139] were [30] which [98] wildfire [128] will [163] years. [109] yellow [91]

[2, 15] [108] [3, 160] [187] [85] [26]

[123] [196] [48] [12, 40, 62, 66, 101, 122, 129, 179, 185] [19]

[190] [21] [120] [146] [34, 59, 105,

107] [147] [112] [75] [63] [69] [54]

[6, 44, 77] [65] [155] [73, 170] [24, 49, 102]

[131] [76] [95] [171]

[74] [145] [162] [51] [9] [164] [151]

[5] [194] [38] [197]

[126] [124, 152] [200] [43]

[84] [195] [28] [144] [133] [8, 27, 52, 104, 141,

148, 154] [142] [132] [60] [96]

[7] [99] [16, 111] [89] [181] [10] [20, 119]

[31] [90] [199] [39] [83] [14]

[138] [56] [32] [87, 161]

lichenometry [1, 23, 110] [79, 134] [103] [72] [106]

[135] [17] [22] [78] [64]

[92] [4] [70] [36] [11]

[86] [178] [37, 55, 82, 93, 127, 130, 159, 168, 174, 182, 188] [80 ,115, 165] [150, 53]

[13] [113] [198] [180]

[18, 193] [50] [167] [46]

[192] [158] [71] [97] [68] [47,

117] [57] [176] [116] [173] [47]

[100] [53] [88] [121] [81, 156]

[184] [114] [33, 58] [25] [140]

[42] [137] [67] [143] [29] [35, 94,

125, 136, 157, 166, 169, 172, 175, 177, 183, 186, 189] [191] [45] [149]

[118] [61] [139] [30] [98] [128] [163]

[109] [91]

[2, 15] 10,000 [108] [3, 160] [187] [85] [26]

[123] [196] [48] and [12, 40, 62, 66, 101, 122, 129, 179, 185] [19]

[190] [21] [120] [146] as [34, 59, 105, 107] [147] [112] [75] [63] [6-] [54]

[6, 44, 77] caches, [65] [155] [73, 170] can [24, 49, 102]

[131] [76] [95] [171]

[74] [145] [162] [51] [9] [1-4] [151]

[5] [194] [38] [197]

[126] [124, 152] [200] [43]

[84] [195] [28] [144] [133] for [8, 27, 52, 104, 141, 148, 154] [142] [132] [60] [-6]

[7] [99] [16, 111] [89] history [181] [10] [20, 119]

[31] [90] [199] [39] [83] [14]

[138] [56] [32] [87, 161]

[1, 23, 110] [79, 134] live [103] [72] long [106]

[135] [17] [22] [78] meat [64]

[92] [4] [70] [36] moraines [11]

[86] [178] of [37, 55, 82, 93, 127, 130, 159, 168, 174, 182, 188] [80, -15, 165] [150, 53]

[13] [113] [198] [180]

[18, 193] [50] [167] [-46]

[192] [158] [71] [97] [68] [47, 117] [57] [1-6] [116] [173] [47]

[100] [53] [88] [121] [81, 156]

[184] [114] [33, 58] [-25] [140]

[42] [137] [67] [143] [29] the [35, 94, 125, 136, 157, 166, 169, 172, 175, 177, 183, 186, 189] [191] [4-] [149]

[118] [61] [139] [30] [98] wildfire [128] [163]

years [109] [91]

10,000 [108]

and [12, 40, 62, 66, 101, 122, 129, 179, 185]

as [34, 59, 105, 107]

caches, [65] can [24, 49, 102]

for [8, 27, 52, 104, 141, 148, 154]

history [181]

live [103] long [106]

meat [64]

moraines [11]

of [37, 55, 82, 93, 127, 130, 159, 168, 174, 182, 188]

the [35, 94, 125, 136, 157, 166, 169, 172, 175, 177, 183, 186, 189]

wildfire [128] years [109]

10,000 [8]
and [16]
as [5, 7, 12, 14]
caches [19]
can [2, 10]
for [4]
history [21]
live [3, 11]
long [6, 13]
meat [18]
moraines [15]
of [20]
the [17]
wildfire [1]
years [9]

FURNESS FELLS

EXCERPTS | 2017

between hills
where wolves played
between two furrows
at the point that
divides
high ground
and low ground
the road lying between
a line of feathers
a tenement now lost

Forget:

ice patterns
on the blind tarn

giant's grave
deep in the moss

the wind's
never ceasing tongue

the deep hole
in the river

Wake:

the ancient river name

the burnt tree stump

the wyrm's cist

the swallow's copse

yarrow
juniper
wormwood

mile upon mile
lift from the opened veins of hills

move with the sun's blood

birch
heather
rowan

mile upon mile
lift from the opened veins of hills

move with the sun's blood

rugged valley
may all your roots
become winged

ON RUIN

2018–19

SEER

On the night
of the first explosion
when the din of sirens
the cries of panic
had subsided

(but the thrill of it
still running our blood)

we saw a fox.

It was white
almost luminous
in the fading light.
And running.
Running down
the street
below.

Down the middle of the empty street.

Fearless.
Full of intent.

*

When they come Virgil had said
you will know it is time. Too late
for anything to be done.
Be ready.

This like any other
of his wayward monologues.
And so ignored.

But in seeing that fox
we thought of him.
God rest him.

And the others yes—
they came soon after.

*

And with them
so it seemed to us
more explosions.

Near and far.

No guessing
as to the where or when
of the next.

Sleep impossible.

We lay on rooftops holding hands.
The stars close overhead.

*

One explosion destroyed the bookshop
in the next street over.

I had visited it
only the day before
with an oblique sense of urgency.
Had lingered for an age
looking for something
other
than what Virgil had told us.

A souvenir
perhaps
from the dying world.

In the end the only thing
I could afford
was a small tattered catalogue
for a museum in the north.

A museum in a city I would never visit.
Probably lost now too.

*

And on the morning
of the bookshop's destruction
I saw him—Virgil—
dancing
in the alleyway
that runs behind.

His movements erratic.
A kind of ecstasy.

Thought it
not in the least odd.
Such were his habits.

But I should have
read the signs.

*

From the catalogue at random:

454—Cupid and Hymen spinning the thread of life.
352—Pan teaching a child satyr to play on a reed pipe.
571—The Virgin's flight from the Slaughter of the Innocents.

*

I know nothing
of mythology.

Despatches from a dream world.

*

Not long after
came Dante
filling his shopping cart
with the fluttering
remnants of books.

Got to keep
some semblance of order
his eyes said.

I helped him a while—
stuffing as many tatters
in my pockets
as in his cart—
all the time wanting to tell him
what Virgil had prophesied.

Too late for anything to be done.

But who was I
to disabuse him
of his faith?

*

586—Angels singing.
588—Angels playing.
367—Night with her children, Sleep and Death.
514—Alexander induced by Thaïs to set fire to Persepolis.

*

Later I returned
and searched the wreckage
long into the night.

Not a single book had been left intact by the explosion.

Hundreds of years of knowledge.
Gone.
Scattered to the winds.

*

From a burnt page pulled at random:

... the whole world and every part of it: You will find it to be nothing but one great machine, subdivided into an infinite number of lesser machines, which again admit of subdivisions, to a degree beyond what human senses and faculties can trace and explain.

*

The evacuations
progressed at great speed.
No time
even for the cherished things.

*

Beleaguered city.

*

And only later
in the increasing absence of people
did we begin to see again.

The green
fullness
of life.

*

403—Cupid charms flowers from stony ground.

*

They seemed to sense our leaving.
Seemed to thicken in the shadows.
Waiting.

*

But some of us
found that
leaving
was impossible.

Each
in our way
found the city
more beautiful
than ever
in its growing
emptiness.

Or
like Dante
felt
a duty of care:
Something that once loved
was now in need of love itself.
We couldn't walk away.

*

But curious
that love
and how it found expression.

In the Old Quarter
I saw a man
attacking a stand of foxgloves
in a waste lot
with a spade.
Screaming obscenities.

In a ruined plaza
a gang of people setting fire to a line of weeds
they had doused in petrol.

*

From another burnt page:

It is opposed to all true philosophy to say that flowers lack their own eternity. They may perish and die here; but they will reappear in the restitution of all things. Nothing has been created out of the Great Mystery which will not inhabit a form beyond the aether.

*

The more
I think
on those words—
those fragments
salvaged from flames—
the more they appear
like one of Virgil's proclamations.

*

Nothing has been created
out of the Great Mystery
which will not inhabit
a form
beyond the aether.

*

A sound and its echo.

But the latter resounding
perpetually
such that it becomes
the more real of the two.

And I can only think therefore
that all this violence
this fire and havoc
is passing.

A moment before an eternity of stillness.

*

I must give myself to the fire.

THE OTHER FIRE

Somewhere
beyond
the city

I am certain there are fields.

I see them sometimes at the edge
of consciousness
just before sleep.

*

I have heard my father speaking to the fire
when he thinks I am no longer awake.

Gently telling it of another fire
a blazing fire made of gorse, fern
and small dry branches
used to season green wood
culled for making the plough.

Not just for the beam
but for the ploughshare itself.
A wooden share for want of metal.

And the scent of this fire like nothing on earth.

*

And the fields
ploughed
year
after
year
until they were left for dead.

And other fields taking their place.
Oats, rye and barley.

And many a ploughshare
cut from green wood.
And the wood gradually cleared
until it became a field too.

And always a fire of gorse, fern
and small dry branches.

*

I have no way of knowing
but I feel that each night
in his mind
my father paces out the furrows
in the ley ground far away
to get himself to sleep.

His breathing becoming regular.
His mind drifting with each step.

And the low fire
smouldering
in the grate.

*

And all the while
the sound of explosions
on the threshold of hearing.

So distant
that sometimes I think
it is only my heart beating.

But I have heard the news on the radio.
It is said they are getting closer
day by day.

And with them fires of a very different order.

*

One night
before the explosions began
I couldn't sleep
and I sat in my bed looking out of the window.

And there
in the lamplight of the street below
a pair of lovers, standing
holding each other in a seemingly eternal embrace.

And then the fire sparked suddenly, loudly
and when I turned back to look through the window
they were gone.

*

I sometimes dream of that other
blazing fire
deep in the night
when ours has dimmed
and the room is cold.

I have never seen it, felt it, caught its scent
but the dream is true to life I know it.

The spark of familial memory, perhaps
passed from father to son.
And so shared.

But like those fields left for dead
I wonder about ancestral memory.

Will it die too?
For I have no children.

No one to pass my memories to.
No one to keep them warm when I am gone.

And so I leave them here.
Gathering in the book's furrow
when you turn this page.

THE LOOK AWAY

EXCERPTS | 2018

I am north of where I was. Go north. That was the imperative. Always north. Although the why of it is no longer clear. Follow the needle. He leadeth me in the paths.

*

The old prayers, unsaid for decades, come back unbidden. Ghosts. Empty conjurings. Dry on the tongue.

*

In a rocky hollow you will find an old shieling. I'll lay me here a while. Safe in the middle of hills. Surely.

*

Each day the rain, ceaseless. The sound like nothing I can tell.

*

What made people climb up into these hills, centuries ago? To a place where even water does not stay, but runs, as fast as it can, to lower ground? What had they done, that they would hide up here? Is it safe?

*

Who is that? Who is there? I know there is someone but I do not see you.

*

I will not give a sign. Touch the horseshoes. Cross yourself. Say His name if you think it will help. He leadeth me in the paths. I will dwell in the house—

*

The pain subsides if I lie perfectly still. But even then I feel movement. Not the dull workings of my own body, but something greater. It is another body, massive and restless, shifting beneath me. Rising and falling. My mind drifts, and although I cannot hear it, I feel the progress of the stream that runs close by. Its thousand veins meeting other tracts of water, seen and unseen. The hills' open pores, fractures and fault lines, flooded with dark liquid. And so my body, filled with blood, water, mucus.

*

Do not stray too far. Stay close to the edge. The waters run deep.

*

The rain ceased a few days ago, only to be replaced by mist. I miss the sound of it. More than that. I long for the din of humanity, machinery, life. A soft bed of noise on which to rest the ears. Anything but this hard silence. This unnatural quiet. I hear only the muted ticking of the clock and the muffled, uneven workings of my own body. Both plague me with their insistence.

*

The pain seems to increase, not diminish. I dress and undress the wound obsessively.

*

Blood, water, mucus. Something has broken loose. Taking on form. I know it.

*

I day-dream of analgesia. A child's sleep. A rest that is the gift of innocence.

*

Perpetual mist. Occasional glimpse of field or hill. No sounds. Everything muted. The world turned to grey. But surely I should take comfort from the fact that I am now doubly hidden. First, by the folds of these sodden hills, which seem to tighten in around me, and second, by this near-impenetrable grey-white cloak. I am an island lost in an infinite sea.

*

Another evening falls. No lights except those in my head. And the images that come from the dark. I comfort myself with the thought that they are simply a delusion. Sometimes I think I see a figure. A darker shadow in the corner of the room. Who there? Show yourself. What do you want?

*

The mist has partially retreated and I venture outside. I see a glacier-ravaged terrain. A narrow valley. The nameless country.

Near-vertical scree-slopes. Banks of burnt-looking bracken. Small isolated trees, bent double from exposure in postures of apparent distress. The rough track that winds its way up from the field-gate, although clearly well-worn from centuries of use, is overgrown and untended. The fields themselves are empty, except for the sunken forms of derelict machinery.

The men have gone, abandoning their instruments. The regalia of deposed kings. And I am their successor. Heir to a land returned to nature.

*

More bearings. The shieling is hemmed-in by various outbuildings, all in various stages of dereliction. The nearest, a low, narrow byre, broods darkness. Shaded by an ash-tree, its doorway—the door itself having long rotted away—grants only scant light to within. Even on the brightest day. Earlier this morning I crossed the threshold, fringed with nettles, only to stumble back, moments later, stinging my ankles, cursing. I returned with a broom salvaged from one of the other buildings and beat back the weeds with a savagery that frightened me.

And my violence disturbed something. A small pale bird, clearly much distressed, rose up in front of me, hovering frantically in the middle of the room, turning ever tighter circles in the air in its vaulting panic. It uttered not a sound but I could hear the beating of its wings, seemingly from all corners of the room. And beneath it the thing to which it seemed tethered. A large, rusted sculpture of twisted wire. In those brief, half-lit moments it felt as if I was at the centre of an awful gyre, that I was party to a premonition of purgatory. The panic was contagious and I turned to leave. Not looking back.

*

The nettle rash has long disappeared but those moments still itch like a newly formed scar. And now I find myself looking in the direction of that narrow storehouse, its tin roof tacked over a crumbling shell, protecting an already weather-worn coil of metal. Why enshrine something already sacrificed to rust?

I try to recall my impression of the wire structure itself. My memory of those moments is distorted and each time the thing takes on a different form. It is as if my mind, doubting the memory, is conjuring it afresh. A sprawling lattice. A contorted human shape. An elaborate snare. A twisted crown.

And more and more my mind is drawn to the bird that dwells in the dark. I can still hear the beating of its wings. What fate binds it to this place, to that byre, and to that rusted coil?

*

Beyond the shieling, the hills loom, lean in, suffocate. The sun is mostly absent. On those rare clear days, no sooner has it risen above one hill ridge than it seems to have already slipped beyond the other, describing a low, shallow arc in the sky. The shadow of that hill—the one that rises steeply up behind the shieling—then creeps across the field to its front, and begins its ascent of the facing slope. It reminds me of a stalking animal. At such times it feels as though the hills will collapse inwardly, and there is a warm afterglow of sunset, like a dim candle in a far-off room. If enough time were to pass I am sure these hills will eventually heal over that great wound caused by ice, millennia ago. I am strangely comforted by such thoughts.

*

Perhaps my ears are becoming attuned to the life that lives below silence. The stream that runs close by. At night I hear it more and more. Running, running. Its dark motion like a chant.

*

Small miracle of dreamless sleep, but it lasts too briefly. I awoke at some point in the night with dead hands. The numbness was so complete that I began to fear it was irreversible. Goodness and mercy. I lay there, hands entwined across my chest, and wondered if it would spread, rather than dissipate. Stealing down my arms, across my chest, up my neck, along my jaw. Perhaps this is how death stakes its claim on the body during sleep? Had I entered that boundary land from which there is no returning? The nameless country. Follow me.

*

Candles but no matches. Spirit stove but no fuel. I am reduced to the life of a wild animal. I might as well drink at the stream, rather than work the wretched pump. I write and rewrite the list. It has become an invocation, or a prayer.

*

This evening I returned from my walk early to discover a beautiful moth on the outside of my window. Surely drawn by some oblique reflection of the sun's last rays. It stayed there in perfect stillness for some time, and I studied it intently through the glass in the fading light. I observed the perfect arrangement of its miniature anatomy. The colour of its camouflage like mottled autumn leaves. One of its hind-wings, I noticed, had sustained an injury. I felt a pang of sympathy. We had both made a flight in the dark. And as I looked past its frail, delicate body to the world beyond, which seemed to fall away around it, I felt a kind of fear.

And suddenly the moth leapt backwards into the void of night and was gone. Such was the intimacy with which I had observed it, that I was stunned by its leaving. Thinking of its small form lost within the vast dark I felt a choking, fluttering feeling in my throat. How can such a thing survive out there?

But later, in the dead of night, I thought this. *Wherever you are, you are free. Beyond reproach. Even if you did not make it, you are free. You have escaped. Nameless and beautiful.*

*

Have I begun to lose myself? I feel my edges begin to blur. The usual chatter of the mind recedes and thoughts come to me that are not my own.

*

—A stone, wet and shining, fresh from the waters. Black and bright at the same time. But soon enough the wetness leaves, and the glamour is gone. Give it back—

*

On what passes for a clear day I sit in the window until after dusk, watching the raking sun drag its last light across the hollow. There is something in the shape of the cragged hill that faces the shieling. I am convinced of it.

Its outline, its contours, the patterning of its drystone walls, the play of shape and shadow, all suggest a form that is other than hill or mountain. And yes, sometimes when I catch it off-guard, it seems to tremble, momentarily. Like a bird. A great bird. Shaking rain off its feathers.

*

More and more, I feel the rising and falling of a great body. The pulsing of its lightless blood. Deep below the surface. I cannot deny it. My body is a single nerve, feeling, feeling.

*

—Nothing is impermeable. There are fractures, planes of weakness, wounds. There can be no resistance. The current is too strong. In the end, everything yields, surrenders, washes away—

*

Go north. Follow the needle. I am caught in the snare of these hills. Unable to fly.

DARK HOLLOW DARK

2019

þe comlokeſt to discrye
þer glent with yȝen gray

discrye] *discry: rewritten, over ſtain, in another hand*
glent] *e: in darker ink over another letter*
yȝen] *n: rewritten*

I

I am in the dark hollow the dark hollow
the dark hollow I am in the dark hollow
the dark hollow the hollow dark
and
I see the seven worlds the seven worlds
the seven worlds or underworlds
and the first world its medium is *fire*
and the second world its medium is *flame*
and the third world its medium is *burning*
and the fourth world its medium is *suns*
and the fifth world its medium is *stars*
and the sixth world its medium is *ash*
and the seventh world its medium is *smoke*
and
the four bodies of water flowing
the four bodies of water flowing
the four bodies flowing around them
the seven worlds
flowing around them
and emptying into the west
flowing through an opening in the sky
flowing flowing
flowing through an opening in the dark
flowing the dark *flowing the dark*
flowing flowing
I am flowing in the dark
I am lost lost in the dark lost I am an island lost
in the dark lost I am an island lost an island lost

lost in the infinite
I am lost lost an yland loste
in the flowing water
the vaulting water
the vaulting lost
the lost lost flowing flowing
and
yes that substance *yes* that crystalline substance
that dwells in the eyes
that dwells in the eyes
and exalts on meeting shining things
yes exalts on shining things
but there are no shining things
no bright things *yes*
in all the seven worlds the seven worlds
the seven worlds or underworlds
yes no bright things left *except her*
no bright things left *except her*
no bright things left *except her*
in all the seven worlds *except her*
no bright things left *except her*
no bright things left *except her*
in all the seven worlds *except her*
and her face dissolved and held in night
when the last leaf forsook the tree
and languid suns were seen
and the goddess of the silver bow
the goddess of the silver bow

on the gude grene hill below
the goddess of silver
the goddess of silver
and the suns themselves were dark simulacra
and the suns themselves were dark
for light is invisible *yes*
for light is invisible
and the darkened waters saw the darkened suns
and when the last leaf forsook the tree *the dark*
and whenne the laste leof forsook þe tree *þe darc*
an wanne þe laste lyeaf fursoke þe trei *þe derk*
an wahan þe laste leave forsoke þe trewe *þe durk*
an wehn þe last live forsok þe trouȝgh *þe deork*
an hwon þe laste life forsok þe truwe *þe deorc*
an wonne þe laste life forsok þe true *þe deorc*
and one þe last life þe goddess of silver
and one þe lost life þe goddess of silver
þe goddess of silver
þe goddess of silver
þe goddess ofe silfer
þe goddesse offe silvire
þe goidesse ofe silfire
þe goddesse of sil fire
þe goddess of fire
the fire goddess
the fire goddess
fire goddess
fire goddess

fire
and
yes and I am touched by *her* fire
yes I am touched by *her* fire
yes and I am fire
yes I am fire
a burning mirror *yes*
a burning mirror *yes*
a burning mirror *yes*
and through the hollow reed *the flame*
and through the hollow reed *the flame*
and through the hollow reed *the flame*
a great body rising and falling
a great body rising and falling
rising and falling
rising and falling
a great body rising
a great body falling
deep below the surface
falling
deep below
falling
a great body
falling
a great body
falling
the body of a star falling
and the earth a star falling

a great bird falling
a great bird falling
a great bird falling
unable to fly
and
that face rising
that face rising
the face that is dissolved rising
the face that is dissolved rising
the face that is dissolved and held in night rising
and gone gone rising and gone
and something indistinct scrawled
something faintly heard scrawled
something faintly heard
climbing
and

II

I am lost I will not be found
I am lost I will not be found
I am lost I will not be found
I am lōst I will not be found
I em lōst I will not be found
I em lōste I wil not be found
I eam loist I wile not be found
I eom lōsed I wele nat be founde
Ih āme loised Ih wole nat bea fund
Ic eam ilōst Ic wile nat ben fand
Ich eom loist Ich whil nat bean funde
hic em lōst hic wiele nat boen fond
hich ame loised hich wole nat benne fond
Ic em loist Ic wile not ben fond
I em lōst I will not ben fond
I am lost I will not be fond
I will not be fond
I will not be fond
am I awake
am I stirring
the murmur of the spheres I hear
the murmur of the spheres
a desolate strain I hear
the murmur of the spheres I hear
a desolate strain I hear
a desolate strayn I hear
the murmur of the spheres I hear
the murmure of the sphers

a desolate ﬅrain I hear
a desolate ﬅrain I hyr
a desolate ﬅrane I hyr
a desolāt ﬅrain I hyr
a desolāt ﬅrayn I hyr
mi re ut si la sɔl fa
a harmony of numbers
mi re ut si la sɔl fa
the sum of all terms
mi re ut si la sɔl fa
the empyreal heavens
and

III

first there is 1
which represents the point
fire
then 2 and 3
the first linear numbers
even and uneven
flame and burning
then 4 and 9
the first square or surface numbers
even and uneven
suns and stars
and the last 8 and 27
the first solid or cubic numbers
even and uneven
ash and smoke
and 27 is the sum of all the former
and 27 is the sum of all the former
27 is the sum of all the former
the sum of all parts
the sum of all parts
the sum total of life
in the seven worlds
the seven worlds
and
sound is not lost by reason of distance
yes sound is not lost by reason of distance
for echoes are divisible by none
yes echoes are divisible by none

in all the seven worlds yes
in all the seven worlds
and

IIII

I have seen lights
in the windows of that wreck'd dwelling
and will see them again
will see them in that wreck'd dwelling
forever see them in that wreck'd dwelling
I have seen lights in the windows
lights in the windows of that wreck'd dwelling
I have seen them
and will see them again
forever see them again
in that wreck'd dwelling
where the wreck'd dwell
that wreck'd dwelling
those lights in that wreck'd dwelling
lights where the wreck'd dwell
yes lights of the wreck'd
yes lights of the wreck'd
dwelling
yes lights of the wreck'd dwell on that *ing*
on that *eng* on that *heng* on that meadow
yes on that meadow lights on that meadow
forever lights on the meadow
faintly scrawled
lights faintly scrawled
lights lights faintly
lights lights lights
and
am I stirring

am I awake
am I a light
a light faintly stirring
a licht faintly stirring
a lich faintly stirring
a lych faintly stirring
below the meadow faintly stirring
deep below the meadow stirring
light of the the meadow faintly stirring
light of the medow
light of the maedwo
light of the mædwe
light of the mæd
lighte of the mæd
liʒte of the mæd
lijʒt ofe the mæd
ligth ove þe mæd
liʒth offe þe mæd
lihte ofe þe mæd
litht offe þe mæd
līte ove þe mæd
litte ofe þe mæd
lichte hof þe mæd
lict ove þe mæd
licth ofe þe mæd
lict offe þe mæd
licht ove þe mæd
lych hof þe mæd

lych ofe þe maid
lych offe þe maid
lych of þe maiden
lych of the maiden
lych of the maiden
and

IIIII

did I solicit thee from darkness
dream thee
call thee
here
thou reivs me of my reſt
who art thou dweller
thou reivs me of my reſt dweller
thou art not a thing of light dweller
thou art a thing of night dweller
breathe in the dark of earth dweller
breathe in
breath of the eternall
breath of ſtillness
breathe in
breith of the eternall
brēth of ſtillness
an infinite breath dweller
an infinite dark dweller
you know why I am here dweller
why am I here dweller
can you tell dweller
I cannot tell dweller
I cannot tell
yes in the great dark dweller the great dark
I cannot tell *yes* in the great dark dweller
I cannot tell I cannot tell I cannot tell
but thou art not a thing of light dweller
thou art a thing of night

yes and all is dark *except her* dweller
all is dark *except her*
and *her* face is dissolved and held in night dweller
and I am on fire dweller
and I am on fire *yes*
and I am a fire *yes*
and I am fire *yes*
throughout the seven worlds *yes*
I am fire *yes*
fire *yes*
throughout the seven worlds *yes*
and in this world of dark
a fire to heather set
a fire to heather set a fire to heather set
yes in this world of dark a fire to heather set
a fire to heather set a fyre to heather set
yes in this world of dark a fyr to heather set
a fire to heather sett a fire to hathir set
a fyre to heather sett
a fire to heathre sette
a fyre to heath set
a fyre to heith sett
a fyr to haith sette
a fyre to faith sett
a fire to faith set
a fire to faith
and
I burn

my brain consumes to ashes
let it rain *yes*
pour on my soul
it will hiss like coal but be never cooler
a fire in the dark
a fire no water can ever put out dweller
the face that is dissolved and held in night *yes*
and each eye too with lightning flashes
pale blue pale blue *the palest of blues*
and within my breast there glows a fire
which thousand ages can't expire
and *she* is enthroned on high dweller
and I crie to *her* aloud dweller
to *her* I crie aloud dweller
to *her* I crie aloud
and must labour to reach *her* dweller
must labour to reach the sky
in my risings and my fallings
unable to fly
in my risings and my fallings
and yet I must labour dweller
yet I must labour
so tell me of the stars *yes*
the vastness of the stars dweller
their risings and their fallings dweller
their risings and their fallings *yes*
their dark and starry motion dweller
even and uneven dweller

their dark hollow motion dweller
even and uneven
and
the ﬅars so small they seem as nothing dweller
the ﬅars so small they seem as nothing
and yet the earth itself a ﬅar dweller
the earth itself a ﬅar
and all are solar bodies dweller
all are solar bodies
and does your blood ebb and flow
with them dweller
does it ebb and flow like mine dweller
does it ebb and flow like mine
on the gude grene hill of night dweller
on the gude grene hill of night
on the good grene hyll of night dweller
on the gude grene hill of night
and the night is wearing faﬅ dweller
and the night is wearing *yes*
to end my lengthened life dweller
to end my lengthened life
to end thy lengthened life dweller
to end thy lengthened life
thy laﬅ life dweller
thy loﬅ life
on þe gude grene hyll ove niȝte dweller
on þe gude grene hyll ove niȝte
the paleﬅ of blues dweller

in þe wyldrenesse dweller
the pale wyldrenesse come
the pale blue waters
in þe wyldrenesse come
the pale wyldrenesse come
the pale blue waters
the paleſt of blues
in þe wyldrenesse come
þe pale wyldrenesse come
þe blue waters
þe pale blou wæters
þe paileſt of blu watters
þe wæters þe watures þe bloue weattres
þe payle wæters þe pāleſt of blu vaters
and
the murmure of the ſpheres I hear
in þe wyldrenesse loſt
an yland loſt
the sky loſt
and its four vaults loſt
in þe wyldrenesse loſt
in þe wyldrenesse loſt
and in the great dark the world no more
the world no more
and I am loſt in darkness loſt
I am in the dark
in the dark loſt
the dark hollow loſt

the sky's great wheel loſt
and in the great dark the world no more
and in the great dark the world no more
and in the great dark the world no more
and in the great dark the world no more
and in the great dark the world no more
and in the great dark the world no more
and in the great dark the world no more
and in the great dark the world
and in þe great dark þe worlde
an in þe grete darc þe wurlde
an in þe greit darc þe weorld
an in þe girte derk þe werlled
an in þe griat darc þe whorle
and in þe grait darc þe whorld
an in þe great darc þe whord
an in þe great dark þe word
and in þe great dark þe word
and in the great dark the word
and in the great dark word
and the great dark word
the dark word the dark word *yes*
and do you not feel it dweller
do you not feel it *yes*
another hand in *darker ink*
writing over your own dweller
another hand somewhere in the dark
writing over your own i*n darker ink*

writing over your own *in darker ink*
writing over your own
and

IIIIII

as blood works in all animals
so water does in the world
and as blood works in all animals
so water does in the world
and as blood works in all animals
so water does in the world
and as blood works in all animals
so water does in the world
and as blood works in all animals
so water does in the world
and as blood works in all animals
so water does in the world
and as blood works in all animals
so water does in the world
and the world is a living body *yes*
the world is a living body
a living body *yes*
a living body *yes*
the world is a living body *yes*
a living body
and that great dark weighs nothing *yes*
the great dark absence of the world
weighs nothing
the great dark absence of the world
weighs nothing
the great dark weighs nothing
the great dark weighs nothing
the great dark weighs nothing

and the gude grene hill weighs nothing dweller
and the gude grene hill weighs nothing
and *thou reivs me of my rest* dweller
thou reivs me in the dark dweller
thou reivs me of my rest dweller
thou reivs me in the dark dweller
the dark hollow dweller
the hollow dark dweller
the dark dweller
the dark dweller
thou reivs me in þe wyldrenesse dweller
in þe wyldrenesse dweller
in þe wyldrenesse come
in þe wyldrenesse come
in þe wyldrenesse
in þe wyldrenesse
a darker ink dweller *in another hand*
a darker ink dweller *in another hand*
and
here thou need'st not dread the raven
nor dread the fox dweller
though need'st not dread
what soul possess'd a dream so divine
what soul possess'd
yes thou need'st not dread the raven
nor dread the fox dweller
thou need'st not dread dweller
thou need'st not dread

for whosoever comes is but a face of *her* dweller
an aspect of *her* dweller
the goddess of the silver bow dweller
the goddess of the silver bow
the goddesse of silver
þe goidesse ofe sil fire
þe goddesse of fire
þe goddess of fire
þe goddesse of fire
þe gōdesse ofe fire
þe goidesse of fyre
þe godesse of fyr
þe goidesse of fyre *yes*
and I am on fire dweller
I am *her* messenger of fire
her messenger of vīre
and
O dweller dear the world is gone
on the gude grene hill dear
in þe wyldrenesse dear
in the dark dark hollow dear
thou reivs me
and
right in my navel I can feel the dark dweller
I can feel the dark dweller
the dark hollow rising and falling
the dark hollow rising and falling
and *thou reivs me* dweller

in the dark dweller
in the dark dweller
what soul dweller
what soul dweller
unable to fly
and yes since you would know dweller
centuries are as seconds *yes* seconds as centuries
and *yes* dweller
you must cut the knot yourself dweller
there is no other way
and *yes* you must follow *her* dweller
you must labour to reach the sky
e'en tho' thou cannot flie
and do you not feel it dweller
another hand *in darker ink*
another hand
in darker ink
writing over
your
own
and
there is no escape dweller
no escape at all dweller
no way out dweller
except the sky dweller
except the sky
for
you are *hers* dweller

as I am *hers* dweller
your name dweller
my name dweller
give it back dweller
give it back
for you have taken dweller
from the sum total of life dweller
the sum total of life
even and uneven
dweller
even
and
uneven
and

IIIIIII

I see the seven worlds the seven worlds
the seven worlds or underworlds
and the first world its essence is *love*
and the second world its essence is *love*
and the third world its essence is *love*
and the fourth world its essence is *love*
and the fifth world its essence is *love*
and the sixth world its essence is *love*
and the seventh world its essence is *love*
and
did I solicit thee
darkness
dream thee
darkness
call thee
here
yes
I solicit thee
darkness
dream thee
darkness
call thee
here
yes
in the seven worlds
darkness
and the four bodies of water
darkness

and the empyreal heavens
darkness
I would rest
darkness
I would rest
in thee
yes.

LANDINGS

CHEMICAL MEMORIES

EXCERPTS | 2019

LIMBS

find the lost shieling
in earthen voices

see the valley edging its days
towards night

and what is left?
overflow of the book

hold back its sea-sick torrent
if you can

dredge the waters
for the limbs of feelings

VISION

and this vision
from the margins
of history

the photograph
draining the dusk
from trees

the map
holding the heads of fields
under water

THE PHOTOGRAPH

she looks downwards
as if expressing
her reticence

her objection
her complicity
her twilight

as if exposing her greenness
her doublings
her dark feathers

as if she sees
the black course of the river
its ruin and its divinity

THE WEAVER'S BURDEN

a woman steps out
of a century of shadows

a bird holds the sky's lease
a river's ends are tied

meanings warp
at the thread edge

of the canal

why cannot
the eye

see through
its weave

hanks of yarn
drawn together

the archive lies

BECOMING

and the moon
is becoming
itself at last

archivist
turn your
heavy-bodied
night-flying
eyes away

the document
must remain
untitled

MORAINE

2020

the moraine is an accumulation of lithic material
deposited by the action of ice

the moraine is formed by abrasion
by coercion & by slow violence
so slow it seems a caress

the moraine has many forms
including lateral medial recessional & terminal
but only one purpose
to remember

the moraine is a kind of language
it is the work of the many tongues & hands of ice

the moraine is not neat & orderly
it is not the work of a single intellect
desperate to be understood

the moraine is the only honest form of writing
its authors are anonymous

the moraine is chaotic
it defies reading sorting indexing interpreting

the moraine cannot be reduced to a singularity
it encompasses everything

the moraine is our past
the ice saved everything & overlooked nothing

the moraine is myth
or rather it contains all our mythologies
hopelessly intermingled

the moraine is salvation
it knows everything that we have lost

the moraine is waiting
for eventually the ice will return

the moraine is our future
we will all be gathered together
indiscriminately

NOTES ON THE

LANDSCAPE, II

2020

CORPSE ACT. The coaled north. Opencast, the oldest layer. Churchways, weave-damaged. Weftsides likewise spun. Rivers, admixtures of wool, sphagnum, amber. Approximate threads. All questions of dates are vague. The map-makers were wrong.

—

SCHALEBY. 'Bȳ near the shielings'. A shawl with fringes to both transverse edges. Sewn together by the weaker contours. The flaps hanging loose.

—

NAMES: Dikehead (XVI.4), Foulsyke (XVII.1) Bullersike, Fordsike, Miresgate, Mireside (XVII.2). Earth hemmed from black water. Common law. Stagnant depths.

—

AGNES WELL: Braided Martyr of the Chaste? Sentenced to fire, but the flames would not touch her. Listed in 1601, but now unmarked. This a great loss.

—

FIELD NAMES: Meadow lonning, Stacks Steads, the Swangs, Round Ingle, *Brihtric's* flat, *Sess*-scales. There is much evidence to suggest antiquity.

—

OUR LADY OF THE SCHELE, 1845. An adult of slender form, a low stature. Seamstress of the black lands draining into the *Sulewaht*. Mud and pillar, thread and needle. Her relics passed to Thomas Bateman, and catalogued:

63.D. *Portion of a garment made of skin covered with reddish hair, and sewed with sinews; fragment of one of the parietal bones; lock of black hair and small quantity of brain in the state of adipocere from the body of an Ancient Briton, discovered nine feet deep in the bog, near Scaleby.*

—

BORDER LAW. The metal is thin, showing traces of wear. Esk, *Isca*, Brittonic: an isolated piece, dug out by peat-cutters. Not an arm of the sea, nor a river, but a distincly limited locus. A point or place: a leather cord round the neck to save from drowning. The entire left-long edge is gone.

—

All roads, bridges, carriageways, cartways, horseways, bridleways, footways, driftways, causeways, churchways. Liabilities for repairs. Public rights over commons and waste lands. Emergency powers.

—

The principles of the Act discussed, redacted. In this present edition (*publication of which has been delayed owing to the exigencies of war-time*), a careful review has been made of the extant texts.

—

BARONY OF LYDDAL. The amount and complexity of industrial wastes studied: coal tips, iron, steel and non-ferous slag, repp weaving, river yarn, crystal twill. Many cesspits contain coarse hairs of an outer fur, the extent and type of which is not recorded.

—

SAMPLE:

Warp, coarse, heavy, adhesive.

Weft, fine, light, sheer.

(Lack of material comparison prevents even tentative identificaton.)

—

The marches of the realms. *Threapland*. Petty violence. Effluent run-off into the *Sullewath Frith*. The making seems on the whole to have been poor. The question of dating shall, at present, be left open.

AND THEN GONE

EXCERPTS | 2020

eorþe þe on bere eallum hire mihtum
may earth bear on thee with all her might

Læc Boc
LXIII

The fear of open spaces is unlike the fear of cities. Threat of distance over proximity. Restless, living movement of leaves and branches against the dull inertia of buildings, of architecture. But fear is fear, nonetheless.

*

Scene. Road, fields, sky. North country, just south of the wall. Early morning, cold. A car, a woman. Alone.

*

Colours. Grey-green, grey-brown, grey-blue. Her skin taking on each hue like a taint. Grey of the road and of the sky. A pathology.

*

Her idling the car for warmth. A sickness in the stomach, or possibly hunger. She cannot tell. Isn't hunger a sickness, after all?

*

Endless pallor, endless muteness, endless sullen resistance to meaning, endless egress of the world from itself.

*

Moods. Bruised. Eyes looking away. Veiled suffering. Aching.

*

And the road itself lifeless. Not a thick, thrumming vein, close to the heart, but something peripheral, thrombosic. Will it wither to nothing in those far low hills, out to the east?

*

No onslaught of traffic here. No heavenly white noise of engine and friction. No joyous scream of life lived with sharpness.

*

But the road's surface still rutted with use. Not from volume or frequency of traffic, but the inevitable slow degradation of time over time. Attrition, receding into the barren reaches of human forgetting.

*

Life itself, almost from the very outset. Rubbing, wearing, thinning. Becoming translucent.

*

And that attrition. That daily incessant working of friction and gravity, a mere feather stroke. A homologue of something far greater. The tender millennial violence of ice and water. Incomprehensible to human thought in its slow vastness. But the land knowing it, feeling it, remembering it. Unforgiving.

*

All that is, an injuring. Gouge, shatter, scar, fracture.

*

Her looking. Up and down the road's flatness. Outwash plain of her own suffering. This residual violence too vague, too distant, for her to apprehend. A fading, yellowing bruise on already jaundiced skin.

*

And so the world somehow occulted. Wreathed. Opaque to her senses. Her blood sluggish. Her thoughts torpid.

*

Wordless anonymity of the rural. Unreadable trees, hedgerows. Blank-seeming pages of fields. Everything known unto itself but revealing nothing.

*

And vertical and horizontal and vertical and horizontal and vertical and horizontal and vertical and horizontal.

*

Sameness becoming somehow both sedative and stimulant. Lulling and concussive. The road a line drawn between the two.

*

Evening. A day somehow passed. The car radio's signal, dried to a thin stream of static, occasionally breaking into sudden torrents of noise. There is comfort in it, nonetheless, and she listens long into the night, curled in the back seat. Voices, humanity, contact. These things are yesterday's vestiges. Tell me again why I am here? Why am I doing this? The image of her mother's tearful face. Go back.

*

Day. The car moving slowly along the road's narrow. She brings it to a stop at a junction. Habitually, she looks left and right, up and down, for traffic, for news. As if on cue the radio spasms into life. There are words but she cannot make them out.

*

Her eyes framed in the rear-view mirror. See her. Something familial between you. There.

*

The question of which way to go. Is this not the same road, splitting itself, riddling itself, offering the deception of choice only to snatch it back, later? Maze of same-seeming green and grey. Deadened beauty of time endlessly spooling in these fields and ditches.

*

And green and grey and green and grey and green and grey. Over and over.

*

Watery call of a curlew in a far-off field. It is remote to her. She cannot resolve that glissandic song into an image of the known. To her it is the shrill, frightened cry of the lost. And yet, deep within the dark fields of her childhood, a bird answers, and its faint voice bubbles up into her consciousness. Fear is another form of knowing.

*

Curlew. Curled beak of the meadow. Circle-bruise of vowels. Diminishing. Dissolving. And then gone.

*

When a bruise fades, what if a mark remains somewhere else? A wound of the skinless skin. How many such bruises should we endure? The fields would tell her, if she would but listen.

*

Each crossroad the same. A multiple of the first. A copy, an instance. Each a variation on the same basal question. She reads the weatherworn sign. Vague backcountry cuneiform, stippled with rust, lichen. Stranded palaeography of the north. And the arrows pointing the wrong way.

*

She plays a child's game of choice with the fingers of one hand. But there is only one way to go. Only onwards. Only forwards. Only.

*

And the straightness of the road. It moves something in her. An eddy in her waters.

*

Morning. Mist. A new blankness. A new anodyne greyness. Forms unforming themselves. Road, fields, sky. Each implicated in the other. The world a narcotic memory of itself.

*

Colours. All that is not mist bleached to blue-grey.

*

She edges onwards. Barely out of first gear. High whine of the engine baffled by the encroaching haze.

*

Distant hills gone. Perspective gone. Earth-flatness a second guess. Perforated theory of light and shade. Proximity everything. Memory reduced to a fine point. Are there even cities any more?

*

Even though it is daylight, and there is no one else on the road, she fumbles on the dashboard for the fog lights.

*

Colours. Incandescent yellow-white of the car's lights leaching away at the greyness.

*

Memory. Drawn to the surface by the lights' heat. A day such as this. The backseat of a car, her parents in the front. Her looking over her father's shoulder at the brightly lit dashboard. His hands on the steering wheel, the left at seven, the right at five. Scent of leather and chocolate. Music on the radio. No. Her father singing. His voice.

*

Her closing her eyes, her foot on the brake. The nearness of it. So close she can touch it. Him. A deep wave of anguish overcoming her. Palpitations in her throat. Pinpricks of sweat. Memory, have you hidden here, all this time, waiting for my return?

*

When her heart settles she opens her eyes again, unprepared for what greets her.

*

This. Close on her face, dilating eyes. Something reflecting in them.

*

A stag. Standing before the car. Enveloped in the lights' corona. Seven tines on each of its antlers. The bright tapestry of its eyes an iridescence. The look of it so unreal and so beautiful it steals her breath. She is trembling.

*

The deer momentarily turns its head, perpendicular. Exhales heavily. In the periphery of her vision other shapes, stepping into the light. Lithe doe bodies, emerging from the nothingness of mist and into her consciousness. Their eyes, all of them, glowing, as if their insides burn with the brightness of suns. The stag stands squarely before the car as the others press close. It stamps the ground with a foreleg. She still isn't breathing. This moment, held for an eternity.

*

The stag stamps the ground again, speaks. A deep, guttural sound. Instinctively she reaches for the dashboard to turn off the fog lights.

*

Her watching as the light of the deer's eyes fades. The dying of stars.

*

The low, vibrating hum of the engine against the stillness of the deer. Moments pass like the wheeling of galaxies. She turns the key in the ignition and the car falters into silence.

*

Scene. The blue-greyness of the car and the woman and the deer. This, the entirety of the world. Their forms softened, insubstantial as memory. Eventually the stag turns and walks slowly away, down the road, the others close by. Each of their forms contracting, dissipating, diminishing, until they are mere bruises on grey-white skin. And then gone.

*

Aftermath. A violence to her senses, her mind. Gouge, shatter, scar, fracture.

*

She sits, motionless, hands at the wheel. The left at seven, the right at five. Scent of leather and despair. She turns the radio on. Thin singing stream of static. Its voice.

THE SECOND CHAMBER

UNCOLLECTED | 2020

I

this
is the poem
you shelved
to resume later

the equation
still to be solved

11

this
is the poem
you tricked
into conscription

that returned to you maimed
shellshocked

III

this
is the poem
you bagged
& drowned in the river

that learned to breathe
underwater

IV

this
is the poem
you shut your ears
from hearing

that clamours
on the threshold of sleep

V

this
is the poem
you locked
in a darkened room

that shakes
& rattles the key

V I

this
is the poem
you left
at the orphanage door

that borrows your tears
when you sleep

VII

this
is the poem
of your ritual humiliation

your song of songs
your birthright

VIII

this
is the poem
of your deathbed confession

speak it now
or forever hold your peace

BURNING

And that phrase scalds again and again.
A fire that will not go out:
'From animals are drawn burning lights.'

Grease. Tallow. Fat.
That inner substance,
their defence against the cold.

It fuelled our
dark
enlightenment.

And they are burning
for us.
Still.

LOW SONG

In a dream I carry a flute made from a
vulture's wingbone. Gift from the Palaeolithic
subconscious. Yet no matter how I try I cannot
bring it to music.

And from beyond the silent world of sleep
a sound wrenches me awake. Outside,
a jackdaw, but not the usual *kak kak kak*.
It is a music like none I ever knew or dreamed.

For three days the bird returns, always at
sunrise. Each time the same low, churring,
guttural song.

And further to the south, the moor, burning,
turns charcoal black, wears a new coat.

Bares its teeth.

DIALOGUE

River, what is your lineage?
I am descended from mountains.

River, is your line still true, after all these millennia?
A cur from the start.

Your mixture impure from the very beginning?
Even since the meltwater.

Diluted, day upon day upon day?
No—the source is endless.

Alluvium, gravel, all manner of sediments?
I contain all things all peoples.

And to whom do you belong?
To you and countless others.

What have we lost?
Your inheritance—each other.

QUARRY

Midnight. The Hunter low, crouched in clouds.
Alnitak, Alnilam and Mintaka, his girdle,
almost vertical. Rising.

To the north-east, the smaller of his two dogs,
and her eye, Procyon, bright, glimmering.
Below the horizon, her sister, the larger,

the more terrifying of the two. Circling. Laying the trap.
And Sirius, her great eye, brightest in all the sky,
hidden, waiting.

*

Wolf, brighter even than Sirius,
when did you split from yourself and become dog?
A binary star. A polarity. One divided by two.

Was it hunger, starvation, or the long footsore miles?
Did you see their fires on the late-glacial tundra?
Did you quench your own nature for a little heat?

But what price that comfort—a heat placed on your own kind.
And did Vega, the pinnacle, the sky falling bird,
finally spill from her perch, and with her the heavens?

PRECESSION

Slow gyre of the celestial night.
Ages pass, civilisations rise and fall, unknowing.
And you tumble and fall,

imperceptibly,
as each day I edge
a little further into pain.

And so I leave my mind's poor rations behind
and crawl beneath you
on the empty belly of myself.

FOREST

I met a man on a dream-road.
He was tall, gaunt, and carried a hunter's spear.

Looking at the waste around us, he asked:
'Can you even dream a forest

so that I might fill it with the ghosts
of the things I kill?'

When I awoke I tried to imagine
a world of trees

but all I could see
were spears.

SONG TO VEGA

Burning bird.
Messenger
of light.

Bright eye
through which
the pole is threaded.

Falling bird.
Your tail-feather held aloft.
Falling.

FISHER

I saw you on the far bank, your head poised a
beak's length from the water's
edge.

Fisher, you have bent the river's neck to your
purpose,
to your quiet grey aeon of hunger.

INCISION

And the bird spoke.
Its single, premonitory cry
cut language

open,
and the poem fell
through its fissure
into the water
below.

*

All language is incision,
separating one iota
of meaning
from an-
other.

But later, when I spoke,
the words seemed narrow
and blunted, like the
edge of a worn-out
blade.

How will I now know
today from tomorrow?

SONG TO EPSILON LYRAE

Blind bird of two heads.
Lord of the birds.

You hold the pole
in your talons.

Do not let go.
Do not let go.

ALBION

The dream of England
is a spark against the wildfire of bears.

The dream of England
is a monody against the chorus of lynxes.

The dream of England
is a vapour against the cataract of wolves.

The dream of England
is a breath against the vortex of leopards.

*

England
you have yet to close your eyes,

you are scared
of sleep,

and of what may come,
bloody and sharp-toothed,

in the silent, raving
darkness.

WOLF-MOTHER

In a dream, my mother, a wolf, is behind me on the trail.
She pauses, drinks from melting drifts.
I wait near a stand of trees. Anxious. A whelp's fear.

Suddenly, a shape among the branches.
A strange, deformed creature. Pitiful.
It speaks to me, says it belongs to no one.

It is hungry and can barely stand.
I see no harm. Offer it food
from our provisions.

But as I near it, something glints
in the fading light, and I sense its
body trembling, ready to strike.

A rattle of atom over atom.

And my mother,
my mother in the form of a wolf,
leaps past me, stakes it to the ground, bares her teeth.

A brutal spark, now extinguished.

That is it.
That is all I remember.
All our mothers are wolves.

THEORY OF ASCENSION

A bird took up from the ground before me.
A child, I watched her ascend celestial threads,
ribbons winding around the pole
that keeps the sky's tent from falling.

'Climb with me through the tiered heavens,'
she said, but when I leapt into the air
I fell, cutting my hands and knees,
crying with confusion, and with anger.

*

All art is born from this first blooding,
from this first and most bitter agony,
when we forget our own true natures,
and briefly think that we can fly.

All art is consolation, as is love.
Love, for want of wings.

THE SECOND CHAMBER

I came to sorrow,
but the soil was already taken,
bagged, screaming.

I came to grief,
but the terriers who followed me
filled it with blood.

I came to tears,
but the river disowned me,
spat at me, foaming.

I came to pain,
but love found its second chamber,
and sang me with lightness.

I came to death,
and she hollowed my bones,
blew through them with music.

I came to life,
and she opened her hands,
so that I might again fly.

OBLIVION

There were
bystanders

on the river bank
of your oblivion.

They saw you
through a haze of self-interest,

but your name
was foreign to them,

and so they looked on
as you passed by,

choking,
drowning.

THE SLOW CATACLYSM

What will I do
on the morning I wake
to discover the world
changed?

An imperceptible
and yet irreparable shift,
a shade,
a dissonance,

like the first time
I looked in her eyes
and knew
she loved me.

HIEMAL

Same returning road.
Straight track from here to the horizon.
I walk it now, as before,
with slowness.

What is the measure of today's losses,
as the year flies its lowest to the ground?
What small lives have ended
their modest pulsing,

unseen and cold
in the tangle
of stems
and grasses?

But as I turn
and walk along the river,
a bird draws itself into song beside me.
A darker stroke, for all the coming

night's thickness.
And yet its black is edged
in a substance that speaks,
if not of light, then a thing near to it.

AFTERWORD

A Flint Incentive is the successor to *The Pale Ladder*, which gathered together the majority of Richard Skelton's poetic writing from 2009 to 2014. This new collection spans the years 2015 to 2020, and presents over one hundred and forty texts from numerous small press pamphlets, poem cards, books and editions—the majority published through Corbel Stone Press, the cross-media publishing house he began with Canadian poet Autumn Richardson in late 2009. As with *The Pale Ladder*, this book omits some of the more visually oriented work from this period. *Of the Elm Decline* (2015), *Thwaite* (2017) and *LASTGLACIALMAXIMUM* (2020) are therefore notable absentees.

The work collected here documents Skelton's ongoing fascination with landscape, materiality and archives. The bewilderingly complex material record of the earth itself, first explored in *Landings* (2009) and, significantly, in *Relics* (2013),[1] is visited again in *Beyond the Fell Wall* (2015). Here, human intervention in the processes at work within the environment, as evinced by the building of dry-stone walls, is set against *other* kinds of agency. The book asks, what can be read in the oblique patterning of forms and marks in the greater landscape—in the traceries of life, both human and other-than-human? Writing itself—the laying of one word after another—is likened to a kind of wall-building, but what happens after the builder leaves, and the wall crumbles? The forces of flux, identified with a kind of horror in *Landings*, are always at work. The processes of reassembly, by agencies known and unknown, intentional and inadvertent, become critical:

> But that sense which was set down in the wall's first laying—is it lost, in being reassembled? Or has a deeper meaning been unveiled?

Beyond the Fell Wall continues the fascination with transformation first observed in *Landings*. Each of the poems II, VI, XIV, XIX and XXIX is reconstituted from an earlier seed-poem; a poem that clearly states the connection between language and landscape:

> to put down words
> about this landscape
> as if they were stones

However, there are differences of scale that produce markedly contrasting effects. In *Landings,* phrases and sentence fragments are recombined in order to generate internal resonances, creating echoes within the text that mitigate against losses—failures of collective memory—perceived in the world beyond the book. Conversely, in *Beyond the Fell Wall,* the seed-poem is atomised and reconstituted so differently that there is no resonance, no unity. The text is at pains to express the instability inherent in the apparently fixed and inanimate lithic landscape of upland Cumbria.

Another development in Skelton's writing is the increasing mythological scope of his subject matter. A key thread in *Beyond the Fell Wall* (though not present in the selections made for this volume) is the *ouroboros*, the serpent that eats its own tail, symbolising recurrence and the never-ending cycle. This eddying current works against the general flow of the book, and against its premise that the passage of time is a revisionary, and ultimately attritional, process. To this it adds a vital caveat: *what is gone may, in time, return. Nothing is ever truly lost.*

This mythological dimension is evident in another sequence, *Ferae Naturae* (2015), which reflects on the possibility of 'plague-cults' in medieval Cumberland, and a return to the worship of horned gods such as Sylvanus, Belatucadrus and Cernunnos. *Ferae Naturae* is unique among the texts gathered here in that it was originally presented as a collection of 'found' manuscripts whose provenance could not be determined. This artistic device allows the poet to densely pack each line with a range of mythological and folkloric references which are then teased out by a series of footnoted glosses. The result is a kind of literary archaeology.

In the context of the associated 'museum' exhibition at Abbot Hall, which displayed the manuscripts alongside artefacts from local collections, *Ferae Naturae* became a multi-layered interrogation of the significance of animal life in both the real world and the human imagination.

When it was concluded, the manuscripts were deposited into the Collingwood Archive—the collection where they were purportedly found—thereby further eliding the factual and fictional, the real and unreal. *Ferae Naturae* therefore became an enquiry into the archival process itself, and into notions of authenticity, representation and truth.

Following the mythological focus of *Ferae Naturae*, a phrase from its text, 'The Cult Revived [in Late Medieval England]' became the title for a new programme of work, initially exploring the deep mythic past of northern England. This ongoing series of texts pushes the recombinatory language of *Landings*, *Moor Glisk* and *Beyond the Fell Wall* to new extremes. At its core, the work contends that echoes of archaic oral cultures can be found in the textual residues of the present. It therefore amasses a 'word moraine' by randomly intermingling sources from a range of subjects, including archaeology, ecology, geology, toponymy, mythology, religion and folklore. This material becomes the *site* for a series of poetic excavations.

The Cult Revived takes the implicit literary archaeology of *Ferae Naturae* to its logical conclusion by trying to reconstitute found fragments into an artefactual whole. The process becomes one of repeated reassembly, with textual shards laid on the museum table in various juxtapositions in the hope that they may represent the exploded shape of *the great lost form*. The outcome, however, can only ever be a work-in-progress; an attempt to synthesise meaning from impossibly shattered elements. *The Cult Revived* opens up Skelton's writing to a broad gamut of forms, short-circuiting personal linguistic idioms and aesthetic predilections. There are fissured and broken sentences, midden heaps of tangled syntaxes and strange, hyper-real or impossible images:

I
objects around found souls
like lingual antlers

II
feathers against proximal remains
grammar: lesser sediment

[...]

I.II
during chamber the resin
the contra of with

I.III
where the body findings
six the the the

Despite the failure implicit in such an enterprise, the word-hoard itself, in its polylithic multiplicity, becomes compelling, and each act of recombining its elements becomes an end in itself. Reflecting back on his previous concerns with flux and indeterminacy, meaning-making arises in *The Cult Revived* out of *process* rather than outcome. Paradoxically, significance continues to occur precisely because there is no fixity, no primal, archetypal form to be revealed. Rather, the act of creation is a manifestation of change; arrangement and rearrangement mimics the processes at work in the world at large: the palimpsestic cycles of renewal in the natural environment.

The action of repeated writing and rewriting exemplified in *The Cult Revived* later became the focus of another work, *Dark Hollow Dark* (2019), albeit recast in a haunted and haunting context. A 'chant in seven parts' it draws on many sources, including the Middle English narrative poem *Sir Gawain and the Green Knight*, and in particular a footnoted gloss on the original Cotton Nero manuscript referring to a word that is 'rewritten, over stain, in another hand ... in darker ink over another letter'. These words become a refrain throughout the text, reflecting on the nature of individual volition and the sense that the stories of our lives can be overwritten by unknown—and possibly supernatural—agencies. Indeed, *Dark Hollow Dark* evokes (and invokes) various numinous entities residing in and beneath the earth, in the sky and stars, and in 'the seven worlds'. Many passages of the poem are hermetically addressed to persons unknown, including someone only referred to as 'dweller', and an unnamed goddess who is variously described as 'the goddess of the silver bow', 'the goddess of silver', 'the goddess of fire' and 'the fire goddess'. The poem itself originates in a previous work, *The Look Away* (2018), a poem-novel in which the mind of its nameless protagonist slowly unravels in the deserted—and yet emphatically alive—environs of an equally 'nameless country'. A place at the edge of maps. In a particularly vivid passage, the narrator observes:

> Perhaps my ears are becoming attuned to the life that lives below silence. The stream that runs close by. At night I hear it more and more. Running, running. Its dark motion like a chant.

This idea of a sentient, singing landscape—of *other* voices—made *Dark Hollow Dark* possible, with its eddying and echoing repetitions:

> and in the great dark the world no more
> and in the great dark the world
> and in þe great dark þe worlde
> an in þe grete darc þe wurlde
> an in þe greit darc þe weorld
> an in þe girte derk þe werlled
> an in þe griat darc þe whorle
> and in þe grait darc þe whorld
> an in þe great darc þe whord
> an in þe great dark þe word

and in þe great dark þe word
and in the great dark the word
and in the great dark word
and the great dark word

There is a sense here that *human* language itself is being pressed to its limits; that its permutations of vowels and consonants are being exhausted in a delirious attempt to articulate something that is beyond language. The result is a kind of madness:

my brain consumes to ashes
let it rain yes
pour on my soul
it will hiss like coal but be never cooler

These lines are adapted from D'Urfey's 'The Frantic Lady', found in Percy's *Reliques of Ancient English Poetry* (Volume II, p. 358), and, aside from the aforementioned *Gawain*, the poem draws on numerous other historical texts to generate its disoriented and disorienting atmosphere. In many respects, textual spolia such as these therefore represent the cornerstone of Skelton's work, from *Landings* to *Moor Glisk*, *Beyond the Fell Wall* to *Ferae Naturae*, *The Cult Revived* to *Dark Hollow Dark*. His writing is intimately concerned with salvage, and with making new through reuse, just as it is acutely aware of the archival nature of the printed word itself. *A Flint Incentive* is therefore both a record of work completed and also the source material for future work; it is the document of a half decade's activity and a repository of texts to further sift through, to arrange and rearrange, to cut and to splice.

1 Republished in *Memorious Earth* (ISBN 978-1-999718-4-7).

NOTES

1 FERAE NATURAE : First published by Lakeland Arts in 2015 for an exhibition at Abbot Hall art gallery. The *Introduction* has been adapted for this volume.

33 THE NOT-FIRE : First published in *Quoin 1* by Corbel Stone Press in 2015. These poems are assembled almost entirely from the Swadesh List—a 'core vocabulary' of 100 words that define a 'proto-language' common to two or more related languages. The list encompasses concepts common to all human languages (personal pronouns, parts of the body, heavenly bodies, verbs of basic actions, numerals, etc.), whilst eliminating concepts that are specific to a particular culture or time.

As each language evolves, through cultural and geographical separation, the words it uses for these concepts will change. Linguists can therefore compare the similarity of words for these concepts in related languages in order to assess how long the languages have been separated.

The list is as follows: *all, ash, bark, belly, big, bird, bite, black, blood, bone, breasts, burn, claw, cloud, cold, come, die, dog, drink, dry, ear, earth, eat, egg, eye, feather, fire, fish, flesh, fly, foot, full, give, good, grease, green, hair, hand, head, hear, heart, horn, hot, I, kill, knee, know, leaf, lie, liver, long, louse, man, many, moon, mountain, mouth, name, neck, new, night, nose, not, one, path, person, rain, red, root, round, sand, say, see, seed, sit, skin, sleep, small, smoke, stand, star, stone, sun, swim, tail, that, this, tongue, tooth, tree, two, walk, water, we, what, white, who, woman, yellow, you.* SOURCE: *Archaeology & Language*, Colin Renfrew, 1987.

43 THE MEDICINE EARTH : Written with Autumn Richardson. First published in *Memorious Earth* by Corbel Stone Press in 2015. Includes material adapted from the following texts: *Handbook of the British Flora* (Bentham & Hooker), *Leechdoms, Wortcunning, and Starcraft of Early England* (Oswald Cockayne), *A Modern Herbal* (M. Grieve) and *Potter's Cyclopaedia of Botanical Drugs and Preparations* (R.C. Wren).

46 THE MEDICINE EARTH : *Swarthened,* archaic. 'Of swarthened and deadened body. The disease cometh oftenest of corrupt humours after the inflammation of the disease which has passed away, the body whilom become swarthy.' (*Leechdoms, Wortcunning, and Starcraft of Early England*, Oswald Cockayne, 1865.)

57 BEYOND THE FELL WALL : First published by Little Toller Books in 2015.

81 THE MEN HAVE GONE : First published by Corbel Stone Press in 2015.

87 THE CULT REVIVED : An ongoing series of works, initiated in 2015, and adopting an archaeological approach to textual archives. The work has been published variously, and is collated as a website that documents both research and work-in-progress: *https://thecultrevived.tumblr.com/*.

The first printed instalment, *The Cult Revived, 1,* was published by Corbel Stone Press in 2016 and contained

'The Dug Head of Young Cases' (p. 119), 'Cumberland Museum' (p. 120), 'The Deep Antiseptic Word Discovered' (p. 122) and an untitled version of 'The Five and Sixty' (p. 124).

The second instalment *The Cult Revived, 2,* was published in a special boxed, loose-leaf edition by Corbel Stone Press in 2017, and contained differently formatted versions of the aforementioned 'The Dug Head of Young Cases', 'Cumberland Museum' and 'The Deep Antiseptic Word Discovered', each with added glosses in the manner of *Ferae Naturae. The Cult Revived, 2* also contained 'The Proximal-British' (p. 140), 'Cradleland' (p. 171), 'The Fells Have Much Mask' (p. 172), 'The Alular Research' (p. 173), 'Willow Commonest Plentiful' (p. 174), 'Of the Man in the Moss' (p. 175), 'The Four Ways' (p. 178) and 'The Rules Set Low' (published here as 'The Rules Set Low (II)' (p. 176). The edition also contained an art print of 'A Litany of Cults' (p. 141), and two poems, 'Archaeopterges I' and 'Archaeopterges II', which were subsequently absorbed into 'Follow the Hare Star' (pp. 147 and 169). Each edition also contained a unique iteration of 'The Unsorted Deposits' (pp. 89–100), all of which are included here in reworked versions.

89 THE UNSORTED DEPOSITS : A series of excerpts from a randomly generated text drawn from multiple sources and subjects, including archaeology, ecology, geology, toponymy, mythology, religion and folklore. This

'word moraine', in turn, became the source for a series of poetic excavations that comprised *The Cult Revived*. In this instance, a *reading/excavation* of each *text/site* is presented below.

102 THE HOLY SHALES : this and others, including 'The Dug Head of Young Cases' (105), 'Scaleby Seascale Furness' (109), 'The Burnt Limits' (113), 'Earth Indices' (115) and 'Mainstream Evidence:' (118), are a series of initial sortings of the source material, which often became absorbed or reworked into later poems.

119 THE DUG HEAD OF YOUNG CASES : Reworked from the earlier poem of the same name, p. 105.

144 FOLLOW THE HARE STAR : Excerpts first published in *para·text*, VOLUME FIVE, 2018.

171 CRADLELAND : First published in *Gull*, 2, 2017.

172 THE FELLS HAVE MUCH MASK : First published on *The Clearing*, 2017.

173 THE ALULAR RESEARCH : First published on *The Clearing*, 2017.

174 WILLOW COMMONEST PLENTIFUL : First published on *The Clearing*, 2017.

175 OF THE MAN IN THE MOSS : First published on *The Clearing*, 2017.

176 THE RULES SET LOW (II) : First published in *Otoliths*, 45, 2017.

182 AN EVIDENCE : First published in *Quoin 3* by Corbel Stone Press in 2017.

183 WHERE NOTHING ESCAPES : First published in *Quoin 3*

by Corbel Stone Press in 2017.

184 STUDY OF SMALL CREATION : First published in 2017 as a poem card to accompany *Quoin 3*.

185 MUSEUMS IN APEX EARTH : First published in 2017 as a poem card to accompany *Quoin 3*.

186 THE RULES SET LOW (III) : First published by *Zeno Press*, 2019.

188 HYOIDOMANCY : First published in *Reliquiae* VOL 7 NO 1 by Corbel Stone Press in 2019.

189 FOUND TRIBUTARY AREAS : First published in *Reliquiae* VOL 7 NO 1 by Corbel Stone Press in 2019.

193 THE FLYING OF TONGUES : First published in 2019 as a poem card to accompany *Quoin 5*.

194 OFFERING OF THE LESSER RITES : First published in 2019 as a poem card to accompany *Quoin 5*.

195 THE BODY FROM SCALEBY MOSS : First published in *Reliquiae* VOL 8 NO 1 by Corbel Stone Press in 2020.

205 FURNESS FELLS : Commissioned in 2017 by Colin Riley for *In Place*, an extended multi-media song-cycle exploring a 'sense of place' in the British Isles The text was later published with additional material in the reissue of *Memorious Earth* by Xylem Books in 2018.

213 ON RUIN : The working title for an ongoing series of texts about imaginary cities.

215 SEER : An earlier version was published in *Hyperborea: The Ashes of the City* by Raphus Press in 2018.

226 THE OTHER FIRE : An earlier version, entitled 'Fire', was published in *Uncolonized* by Zeno Press in 2019.

233 THE LOOK AWAY : First published by Corbel Stone Press in 2018. The text presented here is a series of non-continuous extracts.

235 THE LOOK AWAY : *He leadeth me in the paths*, the first of a number of borrowings from Psalm 23, including *I will dwell in the house* and *goodness and mercy*.

251 DARK HOLLOW DARK : First published by Corbel Stone Press in 2019, the text was accompanied by a series of photographs and handwritten palimpsestic artworks. The poem itself is subtitled 'A Chant in Seven Parts', and is a sequel to, or emanation from, *The Look Away*. It takes as its inception two points of haemorrhage in the original text, the lines 'its dark motion like a chant' (p. 243), and 'thoughts come to me that are not my own' (p. 246). The poem also incorporates material adapted from the following texts: *The Mythology of All Races* (M. Ananikian & A. Werner), *Sir Gawayn and þe Grene Knyȝt* (Anonymous), *Celestial Harmony* (John Frederick Blake), *Garden of Cyrus* (Thomas Browne), *The Secret of the Universe* (Edward Dowden), *The Universe* (The Franciscan Fathers), *Songs and Ballads of Cumberland* (Sidney Gilpin), *Reliques of Ancient English Poetry*, Volume II (Thomas Percy), 'The Spanish Trilogy', 'Overflowing heavens of lavished stars', 'Ignorant before the heavens of my life' (Rainer Maria Rilke) and *The Notebooks of Leonardo da Vinci* (Edward MacCurdy, Ed.).

252 DARK HOLLOW DARK : *Discrye, glent, yȝen,* 'The text here has been altered. This word has been mostly rewritten in dark by a hand using long forms of *s* and *r* different from the main scribe's. A following erasure has been so effective that only traces can be seen under ultra-violet light; the writing seems to have been simply the following line, misplaced.' (*Sir Gawayn and þe Grene Knyȝt*, J.R.R. Tolkien and E.V. Gordon, Eds., p. 75).

262 DARK HOLLOW DARK : *Ing, eng, heng,* Middle English, *a meadow.*

263 DARK HOLLOW DARK : *Lich, lych,* Middle English, *a body.*

265 DARK HOLLOW DARK : *Breith, brēth,* Middle English, *breath*, also *wrath, anger, vengeful spirit.*

265 DARK HOLLOW DARK : *Reive (reivs),* Middle English, *to bereave, to steal.*

274 DARK HOLLOW DARK : *Vīre,* Middle English, *a crossbow bolt.*

281 CHEMICAL MEMORIES : First published in *Landings* by Xylem Books in 2019.

289 MORAINE : First published by Corbel Stone Press in 2020. Originally accompanied by a series of recto visual poems that imitated the destructive action of glaciation.

305 NOTES ON THE LANDSCAPE, II : First published by Corbel Stone Press in 2020. A successor to 'Notes on the Landscape' from *Moor Glisk*, 2012. The poem draws upon various texts, including: *Derelict Britain*

(John Barr), *The Place-Names of Cumberland* (Bruce Dickens), *Annals of the Solway* (George Nielson), 'Olddanske Tekstiler' (Margrethe Hald), *Rights of Way* (W.M. Marshall Freeman & A.W. Nicholls) and various Ordnance Survey 25inch maps for Cumberland, 1850s–1900s.

315 AND THEN GONE : First published by Corbel Stone Press in 2020.

335 THE SECOND CHAMBER : Previously uncollected and largely unpublished.

337 I : First published in *Poetry at Sangam* in 2020.

338 II : First published in *Poetry at Sangam* in 2020.

339 III : First published in *Poetry at Sangam* in 2020.

340 IV : First published in *Poetry at Sangam* in 2020.

343 VII : First published in *Poetry at Sangam* in 2020.

344 VIII : First published in *Poetry at Sangam* in 2020.

345 BURNING : 'from animals ... lights', quoted from 'Garden of Cyrus' by Thomas Browne.

351 SONG TO VEGA : First published in *Reliquiae* VOL 6 in 2018. Vega (α LYR) called *Vultur Cadens*, the 'falling vulture', was the Pole-Star c. 12,000 years ago.

354 SONG TO EPSILON LYRAE : First published in *Reliquiae* VOL 6 in 2018. Epsilon Lyrae (ε LYR) is a faint multiple star system near Vega with two 'components'; the northern (ε1) and southern (ε2) clusters.

ACKNOWLEDGEMENTS

With thanks to the editors and publishers, including Priya Sarukkai Chabria and Kim Dorman, Gracie & Adrian Cooper, Alcebíades Diniz, Laura Elliott & Angus Sinclair, Christian Patracchi, Chris Poundwhite, and Mark Young.

INDEX

BIBLIOGRAPHY (2015–2020)

Books

Memorious Earth (2015)*
Beyond the Fell Wall (2015)
The Pale Ladder (2016)
Towards a Frontier (2017)
The Look Away (2018)
Dark Hollow Dark (2019)
LASTGLACIALMAXIMUM (2020)
And Then Gone (2020)
Limnology (2020)

Booklets

Quoin 1 (2015)
The Men Have Gone (2015)
LINTEL (Vol 2 No 1)
The Cult Revived, 1 (2016)
Earth by Means of the Currents (2016)*
The Cult Revived, 2 (2017)
Quoin 3 (2017)*
Quoin 4 (2018)
Landscapes With Absented Figures (2019)
Moraine (2020)
Notes on the Landscape, II (2020)
Last Night On Earth (2020)

* with Autumn Richardson

www.ingramcontent.com/pod-product-compliance
Lightning Source LLC
Chambersburg PA
CBHW070105120526
44588CB00032B/903
* 9 7 8 1 9 1 6 3 9 3 5 2 3 *